FATHERHOOD

Bill Cosby

Fatherhood

Introduction and Afterword by
Alvin F. Poussaint, M.D.

A Dolphin Book
Doubleday & Company, Inc., Garden City, New York

To my beloved mother and father, Anna Pearl and William Henry—Cosby, of course.

And to those people with no children but who think they'd like to have them some day to fulfill their lives. Remember: With fulfillment comes responsibility.

Contents

I am not a psychologist or a sociologist. I do have a doctorate in education, but much more important than my doctorate is my delight in kids. I devote a part of my professional life to entertaining and educating them. I like children. Nothing I've ever done has given me more joys and rewards than being a father to my five. In between these joys and rewards, of course, has come the natural strife of family life, the little tensions and conflicts that are part of trying to bring civilization to children. The more I have talked about such problems, the more I have found that all other parents had the very same ones and are relieved to hear me turning them into laughter.

Yes, every parent knows the source of this laughter. Come share more of it with me now.

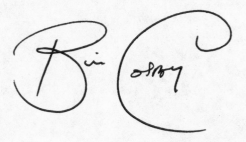

FATHERHOOD

Introduction

by Alvin F. Poussaint, M.D.

Bill Cosby's triumph in this book is to remind us through laughter that models for successful American fatherhood have been changing dramatically over the past several decades. He has sometimes been as dumbfounded as other contemporary dads: "Many men have wondered: Just what *is* a father's role today?" Then he rightly commiserates that the new American father has more responsibilities than ever. Bill recognizes that, though we are closer today to a consensus on the healthy ingredients in a balanced fathering role, many uncertainties remain.

The father's importance in rearing children and his ability to manage families, until quite recently, was not only downplayed but often totally neglected by child-care experts. The general public, supported by pronouncements by leading psychologists and psychiatrists, believed that women, due to "natural instinct," were best suited to raise children and supervise the related duties in the home. Women carried and bore the baby and were physically equipped to breast-feed them, so it was reasonable to assume that they possessed innate "mothering" talents. The ability to nurture children was not only believed to be a woman's God-given gift, but her duty as well.

The father's role was prescribed to be more ethereal and remote from the children. He was primarily conceived as the authority figure who disciplined and taught the children the ways of the outside world. Many famous psychiatrists, including Freud, argued that the mother-child bond was the one most critical to the healthy development of children. And lurking in the minds of many, as a wicked afterthought, was the belief that men, even if they so desired, were not equipped biologically or psychologically to assume the "mothering," nurturant role with children.

No wonder then that, until recently, rearing children has been considered the primary responsibility of mothers. A division of labor evolved, in keeping with strong sex-role stereotypes, that created the model nuclear family, comprised of the stay-at-home mother/housewife and the outside-wage-earner father/provider. Most of us have an image of what motherhood entails, but few of us recognize the different models for fatherhood and their significance in the rearing of children.

More men and women, husbands and wives, fathers and mothers, the divorced and the married, and single parents too, have been taking a fresh look at the phenomenon of fatherhood. As Bill Cosby asks: Just what is it? Bill, who spans the time of the "old" fatherhood to the "new" fatherhood, challenges us with exciting and amusing tales of his own experiences at fathering, to reflect on the dimensions of the enigmatic and complicated issue of fatherhood.

For better or for worse, Bill and I, as contemporaries, grew up under a more rigid definition of traditional male and female family responsibilities. Our own experiences must to some degree color our values today, though Bill and I support the validity of much of the "modern" approach to fatherhood.

In my boyhood home, for example, Papa's chief role was to work: to be the breadwinner, the provider. My mother was a housewife whose chief function was to raise, nurture, and provide custodial care for me and my seven brothers and sisters. Momma relied on Papa, though, on those occasions when we were provocatively disobedient, to be the heavyweight disciplinarian. She would snap, "Wait until your father gets home, you're really going to get it." "It" usually meant a beating, but her threat alone was enough to keep us in check. Fathers were to be feared and respected. "Talking back" to Papa was totally unacceptable. We could "get away" with things with Momma partly because our relationship with her felt more accessible and humane. There was more give-and-take with Mother, while Father tried hard (but not always successfully) to keep the children, and sometimes Momma, strictly "in line."

My father's superior "head of household" attitude toward my mother was also reflected in the way he treated his sons and daughters. Generally, he believed that girls should learn to cook, clean, sew, marry a "good" man, and become a housewife. That was his vision of their fulfillment, and Momma, as a traditional wife, agreed. Papa downright discouraged my sisters from going to college, but two of them did anyway. The boys were expected to work hard in school, go to college, get a job, get married, and, I suppose, become a father like he was. Despite this sex-role typing, my father (and mother too) required that the boys learn how to grocery-shop, cook, clean, paint, and fix things in the house because "a man needed to know how to take care of himself." So there was some degree of flexibility in the children's sex roles but, overall, Papa had the typical old-fashioned attitudes about males and females. But perhaps more significantly, he remained remote and authoritarian with us, sons and daughters alike.

In this traditional father role, Papa was distant and difficult to get to know. It was often hard to relax with him or even to talk to him. But even though fathers were not supposed to be "expressive," Papa occasionally let down his guard and let the warmth shine

through to us. I feel, retrospectively, that he was un-
easy about showing too much warmth and affection
toward us because it might have been viewed by others
as a reflection of a lack of manliness. With the aplomb
of a general, my father was the authority-in-charge and
most definitely the "head-of-the-household." In Bill
Cosby's material, there are images of the besieged father, Bill, struggling to stay tough and in charge but
frequently giving in to his tender feelings toward his
children, striking a better balance than my dad's.

But before anyone starts criticizing my father's approach, let us acknowledge that my dad was not atypi-
cal of the fathers of his day. In fact, in many respects
he satisfied the requirements well enough to be given a
"good father award" because he responsibly carried
out his chief role of dependable breadwinner. We ate
and we had a roof over our heads, and my dad even at
times played with us, argued with us, and disciplined
us enough to keep us on the path of righteousness. In
contrast, I had friends who did not eat well, barely had
a roof over their heads, and had fathers who were absent.

Being a good provider, of course, did not mean that
a father had to raise you to the level of even the lower
working class. What it meant in my neighborhood was
that the father had a job and kept the family off the
welfare rolls. This is an act of responsibility to be respected because if more fathers today were merely
"good providers" and financially supported their offspring, we would not have so many millions of chil-

dren living in poverty. This limited role of the father, therefore, is not without value and certainly is not deserving of belittlement. Feeding your children, after all, is one important way of saying you care.

We all know that feeding a child alone is not enough to produce an emotionally balanced, healthy adult. But Momma was there to provide the missing nurturant ingredients for a healthy childhood. Yet it is difficult to decide in retrospect whether Papa's role was good or bad, helpful or harmful, in relation to our growth: Some of us did well and others not so well. Ironically, some social scientists have reported that many children turn out to be emotionally troubled adults because they didn't have my kind of father around.

Psychiatrists and psychologists in the past suggested that the absence of a "strong father" in the home was sufficient cause to account for the many persons who ended up in mental hospitals or jails. There were some mental health specialists who mistakenly believed that the absence of a "strong" dad could turn young boys into gay men. Most of these theories have now been debunked.

The "strong father" role (which doesn't have to be associated with beatings and remoteness) is not to be totally discounted as part of the recipe for raising healthy children, if it is executed skillfully and given in measured doses at the most appropriate of times, as Cosby's crafty accounts illustrate. The new factor that we must acknowledge is that mothers play this "strong" role too!

My mother was definitely "strong." She changed our diapers, fed us by breast or bottle, cooked for us, washed our clothes and dressed us, did the ironing, made the beds, cleaned house, mopped the floors, did the grocery shopping, took us to the doctor, took us to school, made our lunches, and kept us "in line" with everyday matter-of-fact discipline. She also hugged and kissed us, cried over our successes and failures, and counseled us to respect Papa. My mother waited on my father and knew when not to argue back with him and when to "keep her place." The children sometimes felt sorry for Mother (and perhaps ourselves) as this somewhat mysterious authoritarian figure of a father swept in and out "bringing home the bacon."

However, now that I am grown, enlightened, and a psychiatrist, I can ask the critical question: Was my dad missing something? Were we, the children, being deprived of the chance for a warm, closer relationship with Papa? I can at least speculate that my father's style of parenting required that he pay some emotional price. He *was* missing something by not sharing in some of the everyday trials and tribulations and joys and pleasures of the children, family, and home. It was a loss for the children and Mother, and it was a loss for Father. Papa didn't get to know us intimately because he did not participate in any of the activities of parenting that were considered exclusively women's work.

As I grew up, I felt that I was missing something too. I wanted to feel closer to my father and wanted to know him better. He was not an unfriendly man, but he was too stuck in his image of the role of father as presented to him by the mores of his generation to change. He died when I was in my mid thirties, but he allowed me to feel much closer to him during the few months before his death than he had during my whole life. It was a deeply moving experience. I knew then that, as a father, I wanted to be closer to my own children, for my sake as well as theirs.

Since my father's generation there has been a growing and reviving interest in the role of the father. After many decades where the mother was seen as the exclusive or primary caretaker, social scientists and parents are beginning to reexamine old concepts. The women's movement, in particular, has raised questions about the legitimacy and healthiness of the fixed roles for mothers and fathers in the American family, but men also have been questioning the traditional father role. Social and economic demands, too, have coalesced to put greater pressure on fathers and mothers to modify their perspectives in order to meet the child-rearing demands of changing family patterns, no longer typified by the so-called nuclear family. There are more divorced, single-parent, and dual-career families than ever before. Though the responsibility of child rearing still remains primarily with women, more men have been drawn or forced into new and more active fathering roles. Some men have changed out of necessity, but many others have a new desire to participate and share more directly in child rearing and family activities now that they have been given permission to do so.

Men have been struggling with the unfamiliar demands and challenges of this new model of fatherhood. Many have modified their behaviors to some degree in order to adapt more comfortably to changing social and family patterns. In the process of this change, many fathers have seen new possibilities for their own fulfillment by taking a greater part in child-rearing responsibilities. A new movement has been spawned that has been pushing American men and women closer to the acceptance of androgynous fatherhood—men who take a significant share of nurturing responsibilities for children and the home, tasks that were previously assigned exclusively to women.

As with movements of all types, there is support coming from scholars and a new breed of family and child experts. University professors, cognizant of their previous neglect of the subject of fatherhood, are rushing to restore balance to the parenting role. Recent evidence suggests that the fathering role, or the ability of fathers to support their children's healthy growth, is equivalent to mothers if men develop the attitudes and skills to be good parents. This often requires that they give up old-fashioned ideas about so-called manliness, "who wears the pants in the family," and what constitutes "women's work" as opposed to "men's work." There is perhaps no mystique of motherhood that a man cannot master except for the physical realities of a pregnancy, delivery, and breast feeding. All other ingrained notions about which sex makes the more natural parent are at least challengeable. Men too can be "primary care givers" and can provide "mother love."

Divorced fathers, often sharing custody of their children, want to be more than "Disneyland Daddys" or weekend fathers. Fathers in dual career families who are no longer the sole breadwinners must share more child care and household chores with their spouses. These new requirements for fatherhood have caught many men unprepared because they were reared according to the old ideologies of fatherhood. Nonetheless, some men are changing their old outlook and experiencing wonderment, and often joy, as they assume duties usually assigned to the category of motherhood.

We can see today that the new fatherhood demands a change of attitude on the part of both fathers and mothers toward their male and female offspring. There is a need to eliminate sexism and sex-role typing in child rearing and strive for a more balanced, androgynous approach that maximizes the opportunities and options for both boys and girls. Children brought up with a mix of "masculine" and "feminine" qualities will be better suited to adapt to demands of both the new fatherhood and motherhood.

Many people will continue to ask: Can there really be pleasure for Father in changing a baby's diaper, feeding her a bottle, bathing her, dressing her, and nursing her when she's ill? Can playing peek-a-boo and patty-cake with your toddler be a legitimately rewarding activity for an adult male? Can a father bond with his baby, his child, as easily as the mother can? Is it preordained that fathers cannot be as nurturing a parent as the mother in the development of his offspring? These questions have not yet been conclusively answered by researchers, scholars, or even the parenting public, but the new fatherhood is catching on in many families across socioeconomic classes and among different ethnic and religious groups. No one is sure what the future will hold. Yet, a growing number of fathers enjoy parenting so much that they have become "househusbands."

Although we can by no means put Bill Cosby in this category, the comedic insights about marriage, children, and family in this volume will be recognized by all fathers who choose to be deeply involved in the business of raising children. Bill gives hope to all fathers: "The answer, of course, is that no matter how hopeless or copeless a father may be, his role is simply to *be* there, sharing all the chores with his wife. Let her *have* the babies; but after that, try to share every job around."

Every father—and future father—can benefit from reading Bill Cosby's perceptive, touching, and hilarious accounts of parenthood.

That Bill has taken the time to write this book shows his own commitment to the important role of the father. He has written a very funny book about fatherhood, but his underlying message to all dads is quite serious: Care for, nurture, and discipline your children, and do it all with love!

1

Is Three a Crowd?

The Baffling Question

So you've decided to have a child. You've decided to give up quiet evenings with good books and lazy weekends with good music, intimate meals during which you finish whole sentences, sweet private times when you've savored the thought that just the two of you and your love are all you will ever need. You've decided to turn your sofas into trampolines, and to abandon the joys of leisurely contemplating reproductions of great art for the joys of frantically coping with reproductions of yourselves.

Why?

Poets have said the reason to have children is to give yourself immortality; and I must admit I did ask God to give me a son because I wanted someone to carry on the family name. Well, God did just that and I now confess that there have been times when I've told my son not to reveal who he is.

"You make up a name," I've said. "Just don't tell anybody who you are."

Immortality? Now that I have had five children, my only hope is that they all are out of the house before I die.

No, immortality was not the reason why my wife

and I produced these beloved sources of dirty laundry and ceaseless noise. And we also did not have them because we thought it would be fun to see one of them sit in a chair and stick out his leg so that another one of them running by was launched like Explorer I. After which I said to the child who was the launching pad, "Why did you do that?"

"Do what?" he replied.

"Stick out your leg."

"Dad, I didn't know my leg was going out. My leg, it does that a lot."

If you cannot function in a world where things like this are said, then you better forget about raising children and go for daffodils.

My wife and I also did not have children so they could yell at each other all over the house, moving me to say, "What's the problem?"

"She's waving her foot in my room," my daughter replied.

"And something like that *bothers* you?"

"Yes, I don't *want* her foot in my room."

"Well," I said, dipping into my storehouse of paternal wisdom, "why don't you just close the door?"

"Then I can't see what she's doing!"

Furthermore, we did not have the children because we thought it would be rewarding to watch them do things that should be studied by the Menninger Clinic.

"Okay," I said to all five one day, "go get into the car."

All five then ran to the same car door, grabbed the

same handle, and spent the next few minutes beating each other up. Not one of them had the intelligence to say, "Hey, *look*. There are three more doors." The dog, however, was already inside.

And we did not have the children to help my wife develop new lines for her face, or because she had always had a desire to talk out loud to herself: "Don't tell *me* you're *not* going to do something when I tell you to move!" And we didn't have children so I could always be saying to someone, "Where's my change?"

Like so many young couples, my wife and I simply were unable to project. In restaurants, we did not see the small children who were casting their bread on the water in the glasses the waiter had brought; and we did not see the mother who was fasting because she was both cutting the food for one child while pulling another from the floor to a chair that he would use for slipping to the floor again. And we did not project beyond those lovely Saturdays of buying precious little things after leisurely brunches together. We did not see that *other* precious little things would be coming along to destroy the first batch.

Sweet Insanity

Yes, having a child is surely the most beautifully irrational act that two people in love can commit. Having had five qualifies me to write this book but not to give you any absolute rules because there *are* none. Screenwriter William Goldman has said that, in spite of all the experience that Hollywood people have in making movies, "Nobody knows anything." I sometimes think the same statement is true of raising children. In spite of the six thousand manuals on child raising in the bookstores, child raising is still a dark continent and no one really knows anything. You just need a lot of love and luck—and, of course, courage because you'll be spending many years in fear of your kids.

In talking to audiences around the country, I have conducted my own Cosby Poll, asking parents, "Why did you have children when all your other acts were rational?" And I have gotten answers that almost made sense:

"Because I wanted someone to carry on the family name."

"Because a child will be an enduring reflection of ourselves."

"Because I wanted someone to look after me in my old age."

"Because we wanted to hear sounds around the house."

I don't care how bright people are, I have yet to receive a sound reason that would move a man to go out into the street, find a mate, and say, "I want to impregnate you so I can have one of these."

There was, however, one shining exception in this Cosby Poll. One day I found a woman who was the mother of six children; and with simple eloquence, she explained to me why she'd had them.

"Because," she said, "I kept falling asleep."

Some people call a baby "a symbol of our love," feeling that just the two of them would not be symbol enough. The sad truth is, there are people who marry, grow away from each other, get divorced, and then take this symbol of their love and tell it to hate the other mate.

It seems to me that two people have a baby just to see what they can make, like a kind of erotic arts and crafts. And some people have several children because they know there are going to be failures. They figure that if they have a dozen, maybe one or two will work out, for having children is certainly defying the odds. The great sports writer Ring Lardner once said that all life is eight-to-five against. Well, trying to raise a child to come out right is like trying to hit the daily double—which my father used to do when he whacked my brother and me.

Raising children is an incredibly hard and risky business in which no cumulative wisdom is gained:

each generation repeats the mistakes the previous one made. When England's literary giant Dr. Samuel Johnson saw a dog walking on its hind legs, he said, "The wonder is not that it be done well but that it be done at all." The same thing is true of raising children, who have trouble walking straight until they're nineteen or twenty.

We parents so often blow the business of raising kids, but not because we violate any philosophy of child raising. I doubt there can *be* a philosophy about something so difficult, something so downright mystical, as raising kids. A baseball manager has learned a lot about his job from having played the game, but a parent has not learned a thing from having once been a child. What can you learn about a business in which the child's favorite response is "I don't know"?

A father enters his son's room and sees that the boy is missing his hair.

"What happened to your head?" the father says, beholding his skin-headed son. "Did you get a haircut?"

"I don't know," the boy replies.

"You don't *know* if you got a haircut? Well, tell me this: Was your head with you all day?"

"I don't know " says the boy

Beware, Your Foolish Heart

People who have no children say they love them because children are so truthful. Well, I have done exten-
sive fieldwork with five children and can tell you as
scientific fact that the only time they tell the truth is
when they are in pain.

A baby, however, sells itself and needs no advertis-
ing copy; few people can resist it. There is something
about babyness that brings out the softness in people
and makes them want to hug and protect this small
thing that moves and dribbles and produces what we
poetically call poopoo. Even *that* becomes precious, for
the arrival of a baby coincides with the departure of
our minds. My wife and I often summoned the grand-
parents of our first baby and proudly cried, "Look!
Poopoo!" A statement like this is the greatest single
disproof of evolution I know. Would you like a *second*
disproof? Human beings are the only creatures on
earth that allow their children to come back home.

A baby overwhelms us with its lovableness; even its
smell stirs us more deeply than the smell of pine or
baking bread. What is overpowering is simply the fact
that a baby is life. It is also a mess, but such an appealing one that we look past the mess to the jewel under-
neath.

We even love the messy babies of lower species. One night on TV, I saw a show about turtles. Dozens of them came out of a hole on the beach and they were full of a disgusting slime from the eggs, on top of which was now a coating of sand. A baby turtle has to be the ugliest baby around, with sand all over the eggwhite sauce and arms bent in the wrong direction. Nevertheless, in spite of all this ugliness, I watched that show and found myself saying, "Awwww, look at those sweet little baby turtles."

A baby's cry tells us it is wanted; and so, with a baby we cannot lose. For a new father, this little person is something he can hold and love and play with and even teach, if he knows anything. Without always being aware of it, this father has been loving babies almost since the time he was one himself. Even a three-year-old says, "Awwww, look—baby!" and goes over to touch it. Then we have to teach the three-year-old not to remove the baby's eyes. Of course, this three-year-old is also capable of loving a baby panther.

"Awwww, a little kitty cat," she will say.

"No, a little panther," you reply.

"Can I play with the kitty?"

"No, only lion tamers play with kitty," you say to her.

Yes, a baby is so powerfully appealing that people are even entertained watching it sleep. Just notice how grown people tiptoe to a crib and look down at a baby. Perhaps such a journey finally answers the great question about why people have babies who will soon start saying, "I don't know" and "Mine! Mine! Mine!" and start walking around with their flies always open. The decision to have such a thing is made by the heart, not the brain.

2

With Bouquets
and
Back Rubs

Because It's There

It's love, of course, that makes us fathers do it—love for the woman we've married and love for every baby we've ever seen, except the one that threw up on our shoes. And so, in spite of all our reservations about this scary business of reproduction, we must admit that people look happy when they're carrying babies. The male looks especially happy because he has someone to carry it for him, his darling packager.

But his wife is happy too, because she feels she's fulfilling herself as a woman. I've heard so many females say that they became mothers because they wanted to feel like women, as if they felt like longshoremen at all other times. And so many others have said, "I had the baby because I wanted to see if I could," which sounds like a reason for climbing Mount Everest or breaking the four-minute mile. If a chimpanzee can have a baby, the human female should realize that the feat is something less than an entry for the *Guinness Book of World Records*.

The new father, of course, feels that his mere impregnation of his mate, done every day by otters and apes, is Olympic gold medal stuff. Even if he's afraid of garter snakes, he feels positively heroic. He feels that he and his wife have nobly created something that will last. He never thinks that they may have created one of the top ten underachievers in their town.

Try a Little Tenderness

The male has got to get rid of the feeling that inflating his wife makes him a man, that mere fertilization is a reason for a high five. He has to stop feeling smugly triumphant.

If you really love your wife, her pregnancy is a time to test your attention span. You have to pay attention when she says, "It's moving! Wake up and feel it!" You have to respond as if she's pointing out a replay of a touchdown pass. Remember that the demands of your wife for attention and affection don't come close to the demands that the *baby* will be putting on you.

Not only is her figure changing, but her personality is too. There will be sudden flashes of anger and tears, and from time to time she will blame you for everything from her backaches to the balance of trade. She feels ugly, no matter how many friends tell her that her skin glows.

"If carrying this thing for nine months makes a person look so great," she wants to say, "how'd *you* like to carry it around and put a glow on *your* skin?"

Although you don't have to agree to carry it for her, you *should* make an effort to keep helping her and to keep expressing your love. Make sure that she sits in comfortable chairs; and then help her out of the chair when it's time to leave, or else you'll find yourself in the street without her because she'll still be in the chair, flapping her arms and trying to get airborne.

You have to understand that she has lost more than her mobility and her figure: she has also lost the fun of sleeping on her face. Her new hobby is finding a comfortable position for sleeping, so she needs you to put pillows under her back and head and knees; and she needs your help during her drop into the bucket seat of your car, the car you bought when you entertained the wonderfully silly thought that just the two of you would be living a sporty life, enjoying only each other.

She even needs your help in giving birth.

Almost as Smart as Neanderthals

Before we had children, my wife and I felt educated. She was a college graduate, a child psychology major with a B-plus average, which means, if you ask her a question about a child's behavior, she will give you eighty-five percent of the answer. And I was a physical education major with a child psychology minor at

Temple, which means if you ask me a question about a child's behavior, I will advise you to tell the child to take a lap.

Because we were college graduates, we studied things that people have always done naturally, like have children; and so, we decided to have our first child by natural childbirth. Childbirth, of course, *is* a natural thing: the pains come automatically, the muscles contract and push down, and all you need, as they say, is hot water. Neanderthals delivered children without training manuals.

At any rate, these classes give the father a diploma so that he can attend the birth. And what the classes teach him is how to be a cheerleader in the delivery room: how to say, "Push! Push! Push 'em out, shove 'em out, waaay out!"

My wife's job was to keep breathing, but she had studied how to do this in the course, so she was breathing at the top of her class. By the time we had finished the class, we were well prepared for natural childbirth, which means that no drugs can be given to the female during delivery. The father, however, can have all he wants.

One day near the end of the ninth month, my wife came running to me, breathing rapidly, and she cried, "Bill!"

"Push!" I said.

But then I remembered something from the class: You have to go to a hospital. And so we did, at 120 miles an hour, with my wife moaning all the way.

When we got to the hospital, we went right to the delivery room, where I put the booties on my shoes. Her legs went up into the stirrups, while the obstetrician sat awaiting the delivery, like Johnny Bench.

When the first big pain hit her, I merrily said, "Push!"

Like every man, of course, I had no understanding of how a labor pain really feels. Carol Burnett said, "If you want to know the feeling, just take your bottom lip and pull it over your head."

When the second big pain hit, she cried out and stood up in the stirrups.

"Morphine!" she said. "I want morphine!"

"But dear," I sweetly replied, "you *know* that morphine—"

"*You* shut up! You did this to me!"

And at the next contraction, she told everyone in the delivery room that my parents were never married. Then she continued breathing while I continued cheering from the sidelines: "Push! Push! Push!"

"I don't *want* to push anymore," she said. "Bill, tell them to give me something."

"No, dear, the class forbids—"

"I'm dropping out of *school!*"

"But you can *do* it!"

Meanwhile, Johnny Bench was still sitting there, waiting for the delivery.

"Look!" I suddenly said. "Isn't that the head?"

"I believe it is," he replied.

"Well, go *get* it."

"It's stuck."

"Then get the salad spoons, man."

So he got the salad spoons, the baby came out, and my wife and I were suddenly sharing the greatest moment in our lives. This was what we had asked God for; this was what we wanted to see if we could make. And I looked at it lovingly as they started to clean it off, but it wasn't getting any better.

And then I went over to my wife, kissed her gently on the lips, and said, "Darling, I love you very much. You just had a lizard."

What's in a Name?

Even though all the millions of births are pretty much alike, what will set your child apart from the others is its name. Always end the name of your child with a vowel, so that when you yell, the name will carry. I do not see how a mother can hang out of her window and do anything much with a cry of "Torvald!" A nervous mother needs an "o" or an "i" or an "e" because they last long enough to get the kid home for his beating. That mother also can't be heard by her other son, Dag, because the "g" sound doesn't stretch any better than the "d."

If you must put consonants in your child's name,

put them in the middle, where an "n" or two "n's" or
even four will work, as long as there's a vowel at the
end. For example, if your child were named Winnou,
you could linger on the "Winn" for a long time and
then finish up strong with the "oooo." You could get
past more than two sewers with that name: you could
get a couple of blocks.

My own father violated this rule by giving me a
name that ended in "t," but you have to admit that this
name was an exception. He called me Jesus Christ.
Often he turned to me and said, "Jesus Christ!"

My brother had a name that also ended in a conso-
nant: "Lookdammit." Addressing the two of us, my
father would say, "Lookdammit, stop jumping on the
furniture! Jesus Christ, can't you ever be still?"

My father, however, did sometimes get me and my
brother mixed up. One day when I was out playing in
the rain, he came to the door and said, "Lookdammit."

And I replied, "Dad, I'm Jesus Christ."

In spite of these names for my brother and me, my
father did try hard not to curse, an effort that often
rendered him semi-articulate. Having to squelch the
profanities that he dearly wanted to lavish on me reduced him to saying such things as, "If you ever . . .
because you're a . . . and I'll be . . . because it's just
too . . . and I swear I'll . . ." For many years, in fact,
I thought my father was a man unable to complete a
sentence. I made him swallow curses like after-dinner
mints.

I always corrected my father respectfully because,

although he never gave me a beating, he did often hit for distance. Many times when I was flying by, a neighbor would say, "Tell your father I said hello."

"I brought you into this world," my father would say, "and I can take you out. It don't make no difference to me. I'll just make another one like you."

So my father would not have been particularly interested in a book like this about fathering, although he did like to read. In fact, it was sometimes hard to make him take his face out of a book. One day when my father was reading in the living room, my brother and I decided that we could play basketball without breaking anything. When I took a shot that redesigned a glass table, my mother came in with a stick and said, "So help me, I'll bust you in half."

Without lifting his head from his book, my father said, "Why would you want twice as many?"

3

These Beggars
Are
Choosers

Like the Marines, Be Prepared

In spite of my father's feelings, I presume that you still have decided to have a child instead of a hamster. A hamster, however, would give you more privacy in the bathroom.

Bathroom privacy is something that you and your wife have taken for granted, the same way you have taken for granted a quiet ride in the car, a civilized dinner out, and not having to file for bankruptcy because of investments in toy stores. A new father quickly learns that his child invariably comes to the bathroom at precisely the times when he's in there, as if he needed company. The only way for this father to be certain of bathroom privacy is to shave at the gas station.

The new father also loses privacy for taking naps and for working at home. To a young person, naps don't mean much; he casually takes them in English class. But to a father, a nap is a basic need; and he soon learns that this need can best be met in a local theater.

Whether the father is trying to shave or nap or work, small children come to him like moths to a flame.

"Now look," he says, "I want you to *stop* that. I want

you to go outside because Daddy is working. I've bought you three-and-a-half-million dollars' worth of toys and dolls. You even have a *beauty parlor* for the dolls, which you begged me to buy because it was the only thing you really wanted—except, of course, the motorbike. It isn't that I don't love you. It's just that Daddy doesn't have time for you to rearrange his desk right now. I really do love you—you're better mentally and physically than anything I'd ever hoped for—but right now your hand is on the thing that's causing our problem. That thing is part of Daddy's job. *Your* job is to go upstairs and try to find something in that three-and-a-half-million-dollar room that can amuse you for five or ten minutes. Why don't you take Barbie to the beauty parlor?"

I guess the real reason that my wife and I had children is the same reason that Napoleon had for invading Russia: it seemed like a good idea at the time. Since then, however, I've had some doubts, primarily about my intelligence. I began entertaining these doubts when my first daughter was about eighteen months old. Every time I went into her room, she would take some round plastic thing from her crib and throw it on the floor. Then I would pick it up, wipe it off, and hand it back to her so she could throw it back to the floor.

"Don't throw that on the floor, honey," I'd tell her. "Do you understand Daddy? Don't throw that on the floor."

Then I would give it back to her and she would

throw it again. Picking it up once more, wiping it off, and returning it to her, I again would say, "Look, I just *told* you not to throw this on the floor, didn't I?"

And, of course, she would listen carefully to me and then throw it again.

This little game is wonderful exercise for the father's back, but it is his *mind* that needs developing. Sometimes a father needs ten or fifteen droppings before he begins to understand that he should *leave* the thing on the floor—or maybe put the child down there too.

During this little game, the child has been thinking: *This person is a lot of fun. He's not too bright, but a lot of fun.*

Toilet Training—for You

Except for the cost of the child, which may lead you to consider joining organized crime, fathering is easier today than it was when I began. Take diapering. A father today doesn't have to try to figure out how to fold a cloth diaper, and he doesn't have to keep making little holes in his fingers with safety pins, and he doesn't have to drop the diaper in the toilet bowl.

I do not often get nostalgic about the days when I dropped diapers with their contents into the toilet bowl because I didn't have time to properly clean them off. And then my neighbor would come, I'd forget that the diaper was in the toilet bowl, and when the neighbor went to use the bathroom, I had the kind of moment that encourages people not to have children.

I remember traveling with two babies in those medieval days of cloth diapers. I was always overweight on planes because I needed an extra suitcase with nothing but diapers. A father today has disposable diapers and plastic bottles. The only thing left to invent is a plastic toy that will hit the floor and then bounce back into the crib.

Some things, however, never change. For example, you still have to put newspaper under the child's chair to catch all the food he misses. Eventually, of course, you can sit down and have a picnic on the floor because more food is down there than in the child's stomach.

To the Poorhouse with a Smile

Because you are feeding both the child and the floor, raising this child will be expensive. The Lord was wise enough to make a woman's pregnancy last nine months. If it were shorter, people with temporary insanity might have two or three kids a year, and they would be wiped out before the first one had learned to talk. You know why John D. Rockefeller had all that money? Because he had only one child, so he didn't have to spend ninety thousand dollars on Snoopy pens and Superhero mugs and Smurf pajamas and Barbie Ferraris.

It doesn't make any difference how much money a father earns, his name is always Dad-Can-I; and he always wonders whether these little people were born to beg. I bought each of my five children everything up to a Rainbow Brite jacuzzi and still I kept hearing "Dad, can I get . . . Dad, can I go . . . Dad, can I buy . . ."

Like all other children, my five have one great talent: they are gifted beggars. Not one of them ever ran into the room, looked up at me, and said, "I'm really happy that you're my father, and as a tangible token of my appreciation, here's a dollar." If one of them had ever done this, I would have taken his temperature.

A parent quickly learns that no matter how much money you have, you will never be able to buy your kids everything they want. You can take a second mortgage on your house and buy what you think is the entire Snoopy line: Snoopy pajamas, Snoopy underpants, Snoopy linen, Snoopy shoelaces, Snoopy cologne, and Snoopy soap, but you will never have it all. And if Snoopy doesn't send you to the poorhouse, Calvin Klein will direct the trip. Calvin is the slick operator who sells your kids things for eighty-five dollars

that cost seven at Sears. He has created millions of tiny
snobs, children who look disdainfully at you and say,
"Nothing from Sears." However, Dad-Can-I fought
back: I got some Calvin Klein labels and sewed them
into Sears undershorts for my high fashion junkies.

Sometimes, at three or four in the morning, I open
the door to one of the children's bedrooms and watch
the light softly fall across their little faces. And then I
quietly kneel beside one of the beds and just look at the
girl lying there because she is so beautiful. And because she is not begging. Kneeling there, I listen reverently to the sounds of her breathing.

And then she wakes up and says, "Dad, can I . . ."

Help from a Second Opinion

You other fathers will be happy to learn I have found a
way for you to exploit this juvenile frenzy to own everything that was ever made. At the peak of Michael
Jackson's fame, when I had girls of six and ten who
lived amid Jackson paraphernalia, I discovered that I
could use *him* as a proxy disciplinarian.

"Michael Jackson loves all his fans, but he has a special feeling for the ones who eat broccoli," I said one
night at dinner, and two of his fans quickly swallowed
both that story and broccoli too.

"You girls know Michael Jackson's great big eyes?" I said to them at another meal.

His anti-vegetarian fan club smiled.

"Well, they were *tiny* until he started eating Brussels sprouts," I said.

The problem was that this bond to Michael was also putting pressure on *me*.

"Dad, *you* know people like Michael Jackson," one of my daughters said. "Take us to his house."

"I'd love to," I said, "but he's in Europe."

"Then take us to Europe."

"And what will you do when you meet him? Thank him for the Brussels sprouts?"

"No, I will die."

"Well, I don't want you to die."

"Oh, I'm not going to die."

"Then why did you say that?"

"Dad, it's just a figure of speech."

"What would you do if you saw him?"

"I'd pass out."

"Still no good," I said. "I don't want you fooling around with your mind. I want you to have all your mental powers when you get the Snoopy Porsche."

4

Are They Evolution's Missing Link?

Dr. Spock Never Promised Us a Rose Garden

When a man has children, the first thing he has to learn is that he is not the boss of the house. I am certainly not the boss of *my* house. However, I have seen the boss's job and I don't want it, for sometimes the boss ends up sitting alone in a room and talking to herself as if the enemy were there: "What do you *mean* you don't want to do it? When I *tell* you to do something, you *do* it and you don't stand there practicing for law school!"

In spite of all the love, joy, and gratification that children bring, they do cause a certain amount of stress that takes its toll on parents. My wife and I have five children, and the reason we have five is that we did not want six.

Before we were married, my wife was a stunningly beautiful woman. Today she is a stunningly beautiful woman whose mouth droops and who has conversations with herself. She also sounds like my mother: "I'm gonna knock you into the middle of next week!" The middle of next week, by the way, is where their father wouldn't mind going: I would have four days by myself.

From time to time, my wife also threatens to knock the children to Kingdom Come. If she ever *does* knock them there, she's going to ask me to go get them, and I will not know where it is.

"You know where it is," she'll say. "You just don't want to find them."

You new fathers will learn that almost all mothers are like my wife and have conversations with themselves. These maternal monologists, however, have developed a lovely retaliation. They put a curse on their children: *I just hope that when you get married, you have children who act just like you.* (And, of course, the curse always works, proving that God has a sense of humor.) My own wish is not a curse but a simple prayer: I just want the children to get out of the house before we die.

There is no wisdom I can give you new fathers more profound than what I said at the start of this chapter: you are *not* the boss of this house that you want the children out of within thirty years and you are *not* allowed to give them permission for anything. When one of them comes to you and says, "Dad, can I go explore the Upper Nile?" your answer must be, "Go ask your mother."

Only once did I make the great permission mistake. One of the children came to me and said, "Dad, can I go out and play?"

"Sure," I replied. "I don't see why not."

That was the last time I couldn't see why not. My wife came in and said, "Did you let that child go out?"

"Yeah," I said.

"Well, the next time you check with *me*. He's being punished."

From that day on, I knew my place; and whenever a child starts to say, "Dad, can I . . ." even though it's my name, I always reply, "What did your mother say?"

And even if the child says that she got permission, I still say, "Very fine. Just bring me a note from your mother. It doesn't have to be notarized. A simple signature and date will do."

Ironically, even though the father is not the boss of the house, the mother will try to use him as a threat: "When your father comes home, he's going to shoot you in the face with a bazooka. And this time I'm not going to stop him."

My Wife's Clean Hands

You see, the wives *pretend* to turn over the child-raising job to us fathers, but they don't really mean it. One day, my wife said to me, "He's *your* child. I wash my hands of him."

Where is this sink where you can wash your hands of a child? I want to wash my hands too, and then the boy can go free.

For someone who supposedly had washed her hands of the child, my wife still sounded unwashed to me.

"You go and talk to him right now."

"I certainly will," I said.

"But the thing is, Bill, you always let him have his own way."

"Look, you've washed your hands; he's not yours, he's mine. So let me handle it."

"I want you to be hard on him."

She was singing this song now; but three years before, when I had wanted to set him on fire, she'd said, "Oh, *please* don't. He's such a little boy."

And I had said, "No, burn him now."

Yes, amid all the love, there are still dark threats in any normal family, especially if a man and woman have been reckless enough to allow the joy of making love to lead to something as dangerous as children.

The problem is consistency: there isn't any. New parents quickly learn that raising children is a kind of desperate improvisation. If *I* ever get angry at the children, my wife collects them under her wing and says, "Come away with me, darlings. Your father's gone mad."

Of course, people who spend more than six minutes trying to discipline children learn that consistency and logic are never a part of things. Usually, however, my wife gives the orders in our house. Late one afternoon, I came home from playing tennis, gave her a warm kiss on the cheek, and said, "How ya feeling, pud?"

And she softly replied, "I want you to go upstairs and kill that boy."

"Very fine," I said, feeling pretty happy because *I* wasn't the one in trouble.

When I reached the boy's room, we had that nice thoughtful talk I mentioned earlier, the one in which he could not remember when he had shaved his head; and then, being a father who likes to probe to the very souls of those I love, I said, "So tell me, son, how are things?"

"Okay," he said.

"Is there any problem you'd like to discuss with Dad?"

"It's okay."

And, as every father knows, "Okay" means "*I haven't killed anyone.*"

Such descriptions of his own good behavior do not seem to stop his mother from making the poor boy the target of a hit, and I'm not the only one with a contract. His four sisters—two older, two younger—are also interested in wiping him out. Because some girls are both cleaner and more mature than boys, they had a meeting recently about his habit of leaving the toilet seat up. They conducted this meeting with the maturity that they all possess; and when it was over, they decided to fix him. You see, the two most important things to the American female are man's prevention of nuclear war and man's putting the toilet seat down. Their brother can't seem to learn the latter and may have to pay the ultimate price.

A father has a right to get tired of such constant sibling rivalry. Unfortunately, a father's job is *not* to get tired of what he has a right to get tired of: for example, small people who keep doing things that you tell them not to do, and when you ask them why they keep doing these things, they reply, "I don't know."

It is also possible to get tired of a small person who yells to another, "Will you stop *touching* me!"

"What's going on?" you say.

"She's *touching* me!"

"Look, don't touch her anymore, okay?"

"But she touched me *first.*"

And then you resolve the dispute with wisdom worthy of Solomon: "I don't want anyone in this house to touch another person as long as you live."

Tales from the Funny Farm

No matter how calmly you try to referee, parenting will eventually produce bizarre behavior, and I'm not talking about the kids. *Their* behavior is always normal, a norm of acting incomprehensibly with sweetly blank looks. But *you* will find yourself strolling down the road to the funny farm—like my mother, who used to get so angry that she would forget my name:

"All right, come *over* here, Bar—uh, Bernie . . . uh,

uh—Biff . . . uh—what *is* your name, boy? And don't
lie to me 'cause you live here and I'll find out who you
are and take a stick and knock your brains out!"

All during my stormy boyhood years, I wanted to
get some calves' brains and keep them in my pocket.
Then, when my mother hit me in the head, I would
throw them on the floor. Knowing her, however, she
merely would have said, "Put your brains back in your
head! Don't *ever* let your brains fall out of your head!
Have you lost your *mind?*"

And thus, in spite of the joys that children do bring,
does parenting take its toll on both father and mother.
Mothers who have experience in the trenches of family warfare are sometimes even driven to what I call
anticipatory parenting. They ask a child a question, he
tries to answer, and they say, "You shut up! When I
ask you a question, you keep your mouth shut! You
think I'm talking to hear myself talk? *Answer* me!"

This is a pitiable condition in a mother, but my hold
on my own sanity has also been a tenuous one because
of the behavior of what was created by a few delightful
seconds of sex. Believe me, I have paid for those de-
lights. My three-year-old, for example, used to grab
things belonging to her close relatives and cry, "Mine!
Mine! Mine!" It was a sound that ricocheted through
the house for a while and then went up your spinal
cord: "Mine! Mine! Mine!" If you followed the sound
to its source, you would always find an older child
pulling on the end of what the three-year-old had
stolen, saying, "You took this from my *room!*"

"Why don't you let her have it?" I would tell the older one. "Don't you hear how it's upsetting her?"

Okay, so I *haven't* been Solomon, perhaps because I've felt more like Noah, just lost at sea. But the truth is that parents are not really interested in justice. They just want quiet.

No matter how much the pressure on your spinal cord builds up, *never* let these small people know that you have gone insane. There is an excellent reason for this: they want the house; and at the first sign that something is wrong with you, they will take you right to a home.

When I reach sixty-five, I plan to keep a gun in my hand, for I know that the moment I spill something on my lap, they'll come to me and say, "We're sorry, Dad, but you can't control yourself and you've got to go."

Whether or not I manage to avoid eviction, I hope that these young adversaries appreciate that my wife and I have tried not to make the mistakes that our parents made with us. For example, we have always been against calling the children idiots. This philosophy has been basic for my wife and me. And we proudly lived by it until the children came along.

5

A Guru Would
Give Up Too

Good Morning, Opponents

If a family wants to get through the day with a minimum of noise and open wounds, the parents have to impose order on the domestic scene. And such order should start with breakfast, which we all know is the most important meal of the day. My wife certainly thinks so. A few weeks ago, she woke me at six o'clock in the morning and said, "I want you to go downstairs and cook breakfast for the children."

"But, dear," I said with an incredulous look at the clock, "it's six in the morning."

"You tell time very nicely. Now go down and cook breakfast for the children. They have to go to school."

"But to eat at six . . . isn't that bad for the stomach? I mean, they just ate twelve hours ago."

"Bill, get out of this bed and go downstairs and cook breakfast for your children!"

I would like to repeat a point I made before: I am not the boss of my house. I don't know how I lost it and I don't know where I lost it. I probably never had it to begin with. My wife is the boss, and I do not understand how she is going to outlive me.

"But here's the thing, dear," I said, now a desperate man, "I don't know what they want to eat."

"It's *down* there."

I went back to sleep. I dreamed I was with Scott in the Antarctic, perhaps because my wife was pouring ice water over my head.

"Have you given any more thought to cooking breakfast?" she said as I awoke again.

And so, downstairs I went, wondering about the divorce laws in my state, and I started slamming things around. I had bacon, sausages, and eggs all lined up when my four-year-old arrived, looking so adorable with her cute face and little braids.

"Morning, Daddy," she said.

"Okay," I said, "what do *you* want for breakfast?"

"Chocolate cake," she replied.

"Chocolate *cake?* For *breakfast?* That's ridiculous."

Then, however, I thought about the ingredients in chocolate cake: milk and eggs and wheat, all part of good nutrition.

"You want chocolate cake, honey?" I said, cutting a piece for her. "Well, here it is. But you also need something to drink."

And I gave her a glass of grapefruit juice.

When the other four children came downstairs and saw the four-year-old eating chocolate cake, they wanted the same, of course; and since I wanted good nutrition for them too, I gave each of them a piece.

So there my five children sat, merrily eating chocolate cake for breakfast, occasionally stopping to sing:

> *Dad is the greatest dad you can make!*
> *For breakfast he gives us chocolate cake!*

The party lasted until my wife appeared, staggered slightly, and said, "Chocolate cake for *breakfast?* Where did you all get *that?*"

"*He* gave it to us! *He* made us eat it!" said my five adorable ingrates in one voice; and then my eight-year-old added, "*We* wanted eggs and cereal."

A Law Newton Missed

My eight-year-old was given to me just for love because she certainly doesn't *do* anything. The new American father has more responsibilities than ever, but the children seem to have fewer. Ask any eight-year-old why she can never bring herself to do her chores and she will reply, "But I caaan't. I'm only a little person."

This little person who can jump rope nonstop for twenty-seven minutes says that her chores are too great a strain on her fragile little body. This little person who could ride a bicycle up Mount Washington cannot muster the strength to pick up the coat and sweater she dropped on her way to the kitchen. (To be fair, she may have left that trail of clothes so she could find her way *back* from the kitchen.)

One day, my eight-year-old was fooling around, undoubtedly because I had told her not to fool around, and she knocked over a big bucket of popcorn.

"You have to clean that up," I said.

"But it's so maaany, Dad."

"No, I'm afraid you have to clean it up. We're not leaving it down there for the birds."

And so, she began to pick up the popcorn. She was doing fine for five or six seconds, when she turned to me and said, "I'm so *tired*, Dad," and she started to walk away.

"Come back," I said, recognizing this approach to work from my days in the Navy. "Does that look cleaned up?"

"Well, I did the best I could. It's so maaany, Dad. And my arms got tired. I think I wanna go to bed now."

I am not a physicist, but I'm sure that the theory of the conservation of energy was discovered while watching an eight-year-old pretend to work.

Play It as It Lays

It is no profound revelation to say that fathering has changed greatly from the days when my own father used me for batting practice. However, the baffling behavior of children is exactly the same today as it was when Joseph's brothers peddled him to the Egyptians. And in the face of such constantly baffling behavior, many men have wondered: Just what *is* a father's role today? As a taskmaster, he's inept. As a referee, he's hopeless. And as a short-order cook, he may have the wrong menu.

The answer, of course, is that no matter how hopeless or copeless a father may be, his role is simply to *be* there, sharing all the chores with his wife. Let her *have* the babies; but after that, try to share every job around. Any man today who returns from work, sinks into a chair, and calls for his pipe is a man with an appetite for danger. Actually, changing a diaper takes much less time than waxing a car. A car doesn't spit on your pants, of course, but a baby's book value is considerably higher.

If the new American father feels bewildered and even defeated, let him take comfort from the fact that whatever he does in any fathering situation has a fifty percent chance of being right. Having five children has taught me a truth as cosmic as any that you can find on a mountain in Tibet: There are no absolutes in raising children. In any stressful situation, fathering is always a roll of the dice. The game may be messy, but I have never found one with more rewards and joys.

You know the only people who are *always* sure about the proper way to raise children? Those who've never had any.

High Anxiety

On a recent cross-country flight, I saw a dramatic example of why being a parent is a harder job than being President of the United States. In fact, the scene I saw could have been a commercial for birth control.

On that flight were a mother and her four-year-old son, whose name was Jeffrey. Everybody on the plane knew his name was Jeffrey because his mother spent a major part of the trip talking to him, generally from a distance:

"Jeffrey, don't *do* that!"

"Jeffrey, will you get *down* from there!"

"Jeffrey, now look what you've done!"

All of the passengers knew not only Jeffrey's name but also his age because, as he merrily ran about kicking their legs, he kept crying, "I'm four years old!" I happened to have been spared his kicking my particular legs. Instead, he merely smeared chocolate on my shirt.

And so, as our terror flight moved west, sleep was made impossible by the counterpoint of the voices of mother and son:

"Jeffrey, get down!"

"I'm four years old!"

"Jeffrey, now *look* what you've done to the man!"

"I'm four years old!"

If the passengers had been given a choice between riding with Jeffrey and riding with a hijacker, I know what their choice would have been. The hijacker might have allowed a few of us to sleep; and even if he hadn't, he certainly would not have kept saying, "I'm twenty-three years old!"

As the plane moved west, the feelings of the passengers toward Jeffrey grew more intense. When we reached the continental divide, one gentleman invited him into the lavatory to play with the blue water.

At last, however, there was mercy and Jeffrey fell asleep—five minutes before we landed. When the plane reached the terminal and the passengers began to leave, a few of them took special pains to wake up Jeffrey and say good-bye. And their hearts went out to his mother, who had aged ten years in five hours. Her hair was disheveled, her mascara had run, and exhaustion had seeped into her face. After every other person had left, she summoned the last traces of her strength, picked up Jeffrey, and carried him off the plane, as if she were taking out the garbage.

And there, at the end of the ramp, was Jeffrey's father. He was smiling, he had a deep tan, and he was wearing a clean white shirt and brightly checkered pants. The mother handed Jeffrey to this man and then quietly told him to go to hell.

The First Parent Had Trouble Too

Whenever your kids are out of control, you can take comfort from the thought that even God's omnipotence did not extend to His kids. After creating the heaven, the earth, the oceans, and the entire animal kingdom, God created Adam and Eve. And the first thing He said to them was "Don't." To the animals, He never said, "Don't"—he hurled no negatives at the elephant—but to the brightest of His creatures, the ones who get into Yale, He said, "Don't."

"Don't what?" Adam replied.

"Don't eat the forbidden fruit."

"Forbidden fruit? Really? Where is it?"

Is this beginning to sound familiar? You never realized that the pattern of your life had been laid down in the Garden of Eden.

"It's over there," said God, wondering why He hadn't stopped after making the elephants.

A few minutes later, God saw the kids having an apple break and He was angry.

"Didn't I *tell* you not to eat that fruit?" the First Parent said.

"Uh-huh," Adam replied.

"Then why *did* you?"

"I don't know," Adam said.

At least he didn't say, "No problem."

"All right then, get out of here! Go forth, become fruitful, and multiply!"

This was not a blessing but a curse: God's punishment was that Adam and Eve should have children of their own. And so, they moved to the east of Eden, which was still the good part of town, and they had your typical suburban family: a couple of dim-witted boys. One of these boys couldn't stand the other; but instead of just leaving Eden and going to Chicago, he had to kill him.

Thus the pattern was set and it never has changed. But there is reassurance in this story for those of you whose children are not doing well. If you have lovingly and persistently tried to give them wisdom and they haven't taken it, don't be hard on yourself. If *God* had trouble handling children, what makes you think it would be a piece of cake for you?

The Doctors of Dumbness

In America, there are many experts on child raising who have no children. They are people who have never met Jeffrey, the four-year-old. One of my great pleasures is listening to these people because they are an endless source of richly comic stupidity. They say things like "When I have children, I want them to be very close friends so they can share each other's things."

To be fair, however, I must admit that from time to time children do like to share with siblings. For example, once in a while a brother will try to remove his sister's arm so he can play with it.

These childless experts fail to understand that, for the last nine million years, ever since the first child crawled out of the slime (where his mother had told him not to play), children have had just one guiding philosophy and it is greed:

Mine! Mine! Mine!

Of *course* these small people like to share. The way Hitler shared Czechoslovakia.

The childless experts on child raising also bring tears of laughter to my eyes when they say, "I love children because they're so honest." There is not an agent in the CIA or the KGB who knows how to conceal the theft of food, how to fake being asleep, or how to forge a parent's signature like a child. I have looked it up: the last honest child died in 1843 at the age of ten. He was driven to his death by other children for making them look bad.

6

She's Got
the Whole World
in Her Glands

Prepubescent and Preposterous

Not long ago, my eight-year-old, who is the size of a well-built flea, walked past me singing, "Give it to me all night long."

So I called her over and nervously said, "Give you *what* all night long?"

"I don't know," she replied.

"Then why do you want it all night long?"

"Because it feels so good."

Her fingers had encountered difficulty curling around that heavy popcorn on the floor, but she had the strength to take something unknown all night long.

In the last chapter, I said it must have been an eight-year-old who inspired the discovery of the law of the conservation of energy. Well, at nine, new problems of physics arise, such as trying to hold a glass upright. Have you ever taken a nine-year-old to a movie? It's easy to find one for her today because most movies are made for nine-year-olds. Some, in fact, seem to have been made *by* nine-year-olds.

At any rate, a movie for a nine-year-old is the most exciting thing in her life—except, of course, for avoiding work. The nine-year-old likes to absorb the entire essence of movieness, a procedure that excludes watching the movie.

About ten minutes after the movie has begun, she will say, "I want some popcorn."

So you give her a dollar and tell her to go out to the lobby and get it. When she returns with the seventy-five-cent popcorn, sits down, and turns to the screen, you say, "Do I get any change?" (You have realized by now that if you want to be a father, you had better be prepared to spend twenty years asking for change.)

Well, she almost succeeds in giving the change to you, but instead she decides to roll the quarter down the aisle. She will be happy to retrieve it, right after she returns to the refreshment stand for a soda. You give her more money for the soda and a few minutes later she comes back to you with half a cup. Did she have enough money for only half a cup? No, she had enough money for both a whole cup *and* a bar of candy that you did not authorize; but she spilled half the cup on her way back to you. Since she has spilled out half a cup many times before, you suddenly are struck by the insight that this small person does not understand how the law of gravity affects a liquid. By the age of thirty-five, her father has learned the way to put something down on a flat surface; so at least you know she'll get the hang of it in another twenty-six years.

Often we take for granted that children can do simple things, but simple things can be the hardest for them. Your five-year-old, for example, may fall down at any time, three years after he has learned how to walk. The problem is not an inner ear imbalance: the problem is just that he falls down. It is a talent that is handed down from one generation to the next, for many times my mother said to me, "Can't you *walk?*" My wife and I, however, vowed that we would never say such things to our children. And our children will make the same vow about theirs.

Down Mammary Lane

At eleven, the imbalance in a child, especially a girl, moves from the physical to the mental. At eleven, a girl stands at the window a lot and stares out into space. She is waiting for her breasts to come. The strange look on her face moves you to ask, "Are you all right?"

"Well, sort of, I guess," she says. "They didn't come today."

When the child is twelve, your wife buys her a splendidly silly article of clothing called a training bra. To train *what?* I never had a training *jock*. And believe me, when I played football, I could have used a training jock more than any twelve-year-old needs a training bra. I used to get training knees in my crotch.

Girls at eleven and even twelve are physiologically like boys. And these boys are not ready for them yet;

they are still involved with lower species. They are
wandering around with frogs, sleeping with lizards,
and cutting the heads off flies. The poor girls, meanwhile, are trying to look as lovely as they can for these
little zookeepers.

When these boys do allow themselves to be involved
with girls, it is often to push them around. While the
girls polish their nails, curl their hair, and prayerfully
put on their training bras, they look at the boys and
wonder: *How much longer will they be nitwits?*

And then one day, in the kind of miracle of nature
that Disney liked to capture, it suddenly happens. One
morning, I saw it in my son's face while we were driving to school.

"Dad," he said reverently, "there's a lot of women in
the world, right?"

At the moment that a boy of thirteen is turning toward girls, a girl of thirteen is turning on her mother.
This girl can get rather unreasonable, often saying
such comical things as, "Listen, this is my *life!*"

This remark is probably her response to her mother
having said, "You are *not* going to South Carolina
alone to see a boy that you talked to on the telephone
for ninety seconds."

"But Mother, I've *got* to see him. This is my *life* and
you're *ruining* it! *You're* from the olden days. *Your* life is
over!"

When I heard my daughter say this to my wife, I
went upstairs and packed, for there was no point in
staying with a woman whose life was over.

I did, however, change my mind and I decided to hang around a while longer because my wife is definitely worth staying with, no matter how washed up she may be.

"And where do you think you're going in that Madonna get-up?" she said to my daughter a few days later.

"But the boys are *ready*," my daughter replied. "They're through with frogs and lizards. I've waited so *long* for them to be ready."

"Well, you're going to stay right *here*. You're not going to any mall to look at nasty boys."

"But, Mother, this is my *life!*"

A father who hears this intellectual exchange is rooting for the mother, of course. He knows exactly what those boys at the mall have in their depraved little minds because he once owned such a depraved little mind himself. In fact, if he thinks enough about the plans that he used to have for young girls, the father not only will support his wife in keeping their daughter home but he might even run over to the mall and have a few of those boys arrested.

They Need Ventriloquists

The problem is that your daughter has given her heart to a fifteen-year-old boy, and a fifteen-year-old boy does not yet qualify as a human being. If this boy happens to be yours, he has you in a constant state of embarrassment, especially when you make the mistake of introducing him to people.

"This is my son," you say proudly to some man you know. "Son, this is Mr. Clark."

And there is silence. Perhaps the boy was momentarily distracted by working on a calculus problem in his head; so again you say, "Son, this is Mr. Clark."

"Hello, Mr. Clark," the boy finally manages to produce.

"Hello," says Mr. Clark. "What a fine-looking boy. You're really tall. How tall *are* you?"

And another silence descends. This is the kind of question that you hope will not be on the SAT, or else your son will have to skip college and go right to work at a car wash.

"I said, how tall are you?" says Mr. Clark again, wondering if English is the boy's first language.

But the boy just cannot handle this stumper about his height. He certainly *looks* ready to speak; in fact, his mouth is always half open; but no signals from the brain ever arrive. It's too bad that you can't run a string from his mouth out through the back of his head.

Nevertheless, even though your kids may not be paying attention, *you* have to pay attention to them all the way. And if you really pay attention to them from the very beginning, then you'll know the moment they start to swallow or sniff things that rearrange their brain cells. When Willie Loman in *Death of a Salesman* said, "Attention must be paid," he was speaking the four most important words a parent can know, even more important than "Dad, she's not pregnant."

And with the attention, of course, must be all the love you can give, especially in the first twelve or thirteen years. Then, when the kids start doing strange things under the guise of independence, they will always know that they are loved and that the lines are always open for them to send a message back to earth.

You see, you *can't* wash your hands of them. You have to keep those hands dirty with the kids you love.

People sometimes ask me how I like to spend my spare time. The answer is, I like to go home from the studio and stare at my wife and kids.

Sounds Like One of Mine

Sometimes I wonder if I pay too *much* attention. For example, many parents say that they can tell without even looking when their own child is crying or calling them in a crowd; but I cannot. In fact, I think that every child I hear is mine.

One day in a department store, I heard a voice say, "Daddy," and I whirled around and said, "Yes, honey?" But this honey belonged to another hive. When the child's mother looked at me with a smile, I said, "Sorry, but I have five, and whenever I hear Daddy . . ."

And the woman said, "Daddy . . ."

"Yes," I replied.

"Would you buy me this necklace?"

"I'd love to, but I'm afraid you've missed the cutoff for 'Daddy.' It stops at six."

There is, however, one sound from my own children that I cannot bear: the sound of one of them crying. And the most piteous crying comes not from an injury to your daughter's body but to her feelings. It starts low and then heartbreakingly builds, with fluid flowing from a variety of outlets: her eyes, her mouth, and her nose. Desperately you try to calm her while wiping her face and seeking the name of the person who reduced her to this state. But your plans to kill that person are changed when you learn that the person is another daughter of yours.

"She's *bossing* me!" the little weeper says about her sister.

It turns out that the tragedy has been caused by her sister stopping her from putting on one of her mother's silk scarves. And the very telling of this awful tale now triggers even more tears.

At once, you turn from the dripping victim and call in the older sister, that dastardly girl.

"But Mom says you can't *wear* that," the sister tells the little one.

"I *know*, but you still can't boss me and snatch it away," the little one says with her own wondrous logic.

And she underscores her point by starting to cry again and flinging herself on the bed. She has lost so much fluid that you fear she needs an IV of saline solution.

After thanking the older sister for her information, you quickly go to the mother and plead the little one's case.

"Our youngest daughter is having a nervous breakdown because she wants to wear your scarf for a little while," you say. "Is there any particular reason why she can't wear it?"

The mother now gives you a particular reason: because she says so. As you return to the child, you are filled by anguish over her plight. She, however, not only has stopped crying, but she is happily playing with something else. Because fathers shift gears much more slowly than crying children, you will be brooding about this whole business for another hour or so, long after your little one has forgotten it. Call it the anguish gap. Call it just another part of being a father: trying to catch up to both misery and joy.

7

The Fourth R
Is Ridiculousness

No Problem, But It Needs a Solution

When your fifteen-year-old son does speak, he often says one of two things: either "Okay," which, as we know, means "I haven't killed anyone," or "No problem."

"No problem" has been my son's philosophy of life. Two years ago, he was one of the top ten under-achievers in our state and whenever you asked him how he was doing in school, he always said, with simple eloquence, "No problem." And, of course, his answer made sense: there *was* no problem, no confusion about how he was doing. He had failed everything; and what he hadn't failed, he hadn't taken yet. (Undoubtedly, F's had even been penciled in for next year.) He had even failed *English*.

His failing his native tongue piqued my curiosity, so I said, "How can you fail English?"

"Yeah," he replied.

Hoping to get an answer that had something to do with the question, I said again, "Please tell me: how can you fail English?"

"I don't know," he said.

"Son, you didn't really fail *English*, did you? You failed handing in reports on time, right? Because you can understand people who speak English, can't you? And when you talk, *they* can understand *you*, can't they? So the teacher *understood* what you had written but just didn't care for the way you put it, right? You just failed *organization*, right? I mean, the teacher who failed you in English also said, 'He can do the work,' right? It's just that you don't *want* to do it yet. And all it'll take is maybe leaving you out in the wilderness with no food or money in the middle of winter. Just a dime to make a collect call saying that you're ready to study."

"No problem," he said.

The Five Worst Words

He can do the work.

I talked before about the four most important words a parent can hear. Well, *these* are the five *worst* words a parent can hear: *He can do the work.* If the teachers could keep themselves from putting these words on report cards, all would be fine because the kids don't *look* that smart. When you see them walking around the house, they look as though their entire body of knowledge is the location of the refrigerator. And so, if the teacher said on the report card, *This kid is a total and hopeless jackass who may have trouble learning his zip code*, then the parent wouldn't be teased by the possibility of scholastic success.

This is a boy whose mind goes out of neutral only when giving reasons why he didn't turn in his work on time. On one occasion, he said that the dog ate his book report; and another time he said that he was robbed of his homework. The thief took no money, just the homework.

He called me the other day, my splendidly underachieving son. He is in a fine school now with four teachers for every child—two in front and two in back. He called to give me a detailed report on his progress to date.

"No problem," he said.

Then, however, he suddenly waxed articulate and said, "Dad, I want to be able to control my own destiny."

"Oh, God," I said, "does this mean LSD?"

And I had visions of him going airborne in his room. He probably would have wanted a movie on the flight, too.

Your Own Grades

When your child is struggling in school, you have such a strong desire to help that you often find it easier just to do the work yourself than to use a middleman. A few weeks ago my daughter came to me and said, "Dad, I'm in a bind. I've got to do this paper right away."

"All right," I said, "what's your plan of work?"

"You type it for me."

Once again, I typed her paper; but when I had finished and looked at the work, I said, "I'm afraid there's just one problem."

"What's that?" she said.

"This is awful. As your secretary, I can't let you turn this in."

Needless to say, I rewrote it for her and I picked up a B minus. I would have had a B plus if I hadn't misspelled all those words.

And so, I've now done high school at least twice, probably closer to three times; and I've gone through college a couple of times, too. Sending your daughter to college is one thing, but going to college *with* her is a wonderful way for the two of you to grow closer together.

Although we try hard to inspire our kids to do good work on their own, the motivation for such work always has to come from inside them; and if the kids really don't want to study, don't want to achieve, then we must not feel guilty; we are not at fault. You can make your boy come home from school at three-thirty, but you can't go up to his room and stand there to make sure that he immerses himself in the three R's instead of rock and roll.

The problem is one that every parent knows well: no matter what you tell your child to do, he will always do the opposite. This is Cosby's First Law of Intergenerational Perversity. Maybe the way to get a child to do his schoolwork is to say, "I want you to forget about school and spend the next two weeks at the mall."

No, Cosby's Law would be suspended for that. He would *go* to the mall and he would take your Visa card, too.

And here's the whole challenge of being a parent. Even though your kids will consistently do the exact opposite of what you tell them to do, you have to keep loving them just as much. To any question about your response to a child's strange behavior, there is really just one answer: give them love. I make a lot of money and I've given a lot of it to charities, but I've given all of myself to my wife and the kids, and that's the best donation I'll ever make.

Try Indirection and Prayer

No matter how much love you give, of course, you will still have the endlessly maddening job of trying to get your child to do the right thing, both in and out of school. For example, there is no moment in parenting

more distressing than when your child goes to someone else's home and forgets to call you. It is not easy to
forget such a call because you have told him nine times
that he should make it; but the achievement of forget-
ting is one that he manages nonetheless.

One weekend, my oldest daughter left home to visit
a friend who lived about thirty miles away. I missed
her terribly, of course, and I also wondered if she had
arrived safely, so I called her.

"Hey, Dad," she said, warming my heart by remembering who I was.

"Honey, I just wanted to make sure you were safe,"
I said.

"Of *course.*"

"But I didn't *know.*"

"Oh, yeah. I forgot."

"Well, the next time I'll just leave it up to the State
Police, okay? I'll just have them call me and let me
know that you arrived. I'm sure they have a service
like that for frantic fathers."

"Oh, Dad, that's not fair."

"True. I told you less than ten times to call me, so
you may have missed the message. You see, all I want
to know is that you got someplace safely—someplace
far away, that is. It doesn't count for local trips. I
mean, you don't have to call and say, 'Dad, I made it to
the bank.' Wait a minute—*I* see what happened: you
forgot our number."

But then I realized it was unlikely she'd forgotten
our number because it was the number she called for

money. In fact, those trips to the bank are just walks to my den.

What is equally maddening about the visit of your child to some distant home is the call you get from the mother or father there telling you how lovely and helpful your child has been.

"I just can't tell you what a polite young gentleman he is," the mother says. "He straightened his room and he made his bed and he even offered to do the dishes."

At moments like these, you truly feel that you have fallen down the rabbit hole.

8

Speak Loudly
and Carry
a Small Stick

Batter Up

Let me repeat: *nothing* is harder for a parent than getting your kids to do the right thing. There is such a rich variety of ways for you to fail: by using threats, by using bribery, by using reason, by using example, by using blackmail, or by pleading for mercy. Walk into any bus terminal in America and you will see men on benches poignantly staring into space with the looks of generals who have just surrendered. They are fathers who have run out of ways to get their children to do the right thing, for such a feat is even harder than getting my daughter to remember her own telephone number.

I succeeded once. It happened after my son, who was twelve at the time, had sent me on a trip to the end of my rope. He had taken up a new hobby: lying; and he was doing it so well that he was raising it to an art. Disturbing letters were coming from school—disturbing to me, not to him, for he was full of the feeling that he could get away with anything; and he was right.

"No longer are we going to *ask* you to do something," I told him one day, "we're going to *tell* you that you'd better do it. This is the law of our house: you do what we *tell* you to do. Thomas Jefferson will pardon me, but you're the one American who isn't ready for freedom. You don't function well with it. Do you understand?"

"Yes, Dad," he said.

A few days later, I called from Las Vegas and learned from my wife that this law of the house had been broken. I was hardly taken by surprise to learn that the outlaw was my son.

"Why didn't you do what you were told?" I said to him on the phone. "This is the second time I've had to tell you, and your mother's very upset. The school also says you're not coming in with the work."

"Well, I just don't feel like doing it," he said.

"Very well. How does this idea strike you? When I come home on Thursday, I'm going to kick your butt."

Now I know that many distinguished psychologists feel that kicking butt is a reversion to the Stone Age. But kids may have paid more attention in the Stone Age. When a father said, "No shrinking heads this week," his boy may have listened.

On Thursday, I came home, but I couldn't find the boy. He didn't make an appearance at dinner, and when I awoke the next morning, he still wasn't there. So I assembled my staff and solemnly said, "Ladies, where is my son?"

"He's around here *somewhere*," one of my daughters said. They were the French underground hiding one of their heroes from the Nazis.

At last, just before dinner, he entered the house, tired of wandering in the wilderness.

"Young man," I said, "I told you that when I came home, I would kick your behind."

"Yes, Dad," he replied.

"And you know why, don't you?"

"Yes, Dad."

"Then let's go over to the barn."

He may have been slow in his studies, but by now he must have suspected that I wasn't planning a lesson in animal husbandry. When we reached the barn, I said, "Son, we are now going to have a little talk about breaking the law and lying."

As the boy watched me roll up my sleeves, his usual cool gave way to fear, even though I was a father with absolutely no batting average: I had never before hit him or any of the other children. Was I making a mistake now? If so, it would just be mistake number nine thousand, seven hundred, and sixty-three.

"Dad, I know I was wrong," he said, "and I'm really sorry for what I did. I'll never do it again."

"I appreciate your saying that," I said, "and I love you; but I made a promise to you and you wouldn't respect me if I broke it."

"Oh, Dad, *I'd* respect you—I'd respect you like crazy!"

"Son, it's too late."

"It's *never* too late!"

He was reaching heights of legal eloquence, which

didn't help him because I've often wanted to hit law-yers, too.

"Just turn around," I said. "I want you to know that this is a form of punishment I truly do not believe in."

"I hate to see you go against your *principles*, Dad."

"I can make an exception. I also won't say that this will hurt me more than it will hurt you. That would be true only if I turned around and let you hit *me*. This is simply a barbaric form of punishment, but it happens to match your barbaric behavior."

And then I hit him. He rose up on his toes in the point position and the tears began.

"Now do you understand my point about never lying again?" I said.

"Oh *yes*, Dad!" he said. "I've never understood it better."

"Fine. Now you can go."

He turned around to leave and I hit him again. When he turned back to me with a look of having been betrayed, I said, "I'm sorry; I lied. Do you ever want me to lie to you again?"

"No, Dad," he said.

And to this day, he has not lied again to me or my wife. Moreover, we received a letter from his school taking credit for having done a wonderful job on our son. I'm glad I had been able to supplement this work by the school with my own parent-student conference in the barn.

Could I have done anything else to put him on the road to righteousness? My wife and I spent long hours pondering this question. The problem was that the reservoir was empty: we had tried all the civilized ways to redirect him, but he kept feeling he could wait us out and get away with anything. And we loved him too much to let him go on thinking that.

The week after our trip to the barn, a friend of mine, Dr. Eddie Newman, said something that clicked with the boy.

"My boy is having his problems being a serious student," I told Eddie.

"Well, your studying is very important," Eddie said, while the boy sat smiling a smile that said: an old person is about to hand out some Wisdom. Could this please be over fast? "You know, a jet plane burns its greatest energy taking off; but once it reaches its cruising altitude, it burns less fuel. Just like studying. If you're constantly taking off and landing, you're going to burn more fuel as opposed to taking off and staying up there and maintaining that altitude."

A few days later, I ran into my son in the house. (He was around a lot more now that he knew the designated hitter had retired.)

"How's school?" I said.

Without a word, he raised his arm and laid his palm down and flat like a plane that had leveled off. He suddenly knew it was the only way to fly.

There are many good moments in fathering, but few better than that.

Pride and Prejudice

It is easy for a father to say that a child who will not behave is not his problem but the problem of the boss of the house, his wife. Real fatherhood, however, means total acceptance of the child for better or worse; and once in a while, as you have seen, better comes along.

Many fathers feel that one of these better moments is sitting in the stands of a stadium and watching your son carry a football to glory. As a former Temple halfback on a truly nondescript football team, I've been guilty of such quaint machismo, such yearning to see a son who is my reincarnation on a football field, such desire to see a projection of myself get a second chance to break a leg. I have dreamed of sitting in the stands and having a man beside me point to something streaking down the field and say, "Is that your son?"

"Yes, that's my boy," I'll reply. "The galloping ghost with the name Cosby on his back. I'd be doing the galloping myself, but the team has a funny rule about using postgraduate students of forty-eight, so I decided to give the boy the business. He's now in charge of running for touchdowns."

Training my son to succeed in the business has guaranteed that there will be no more trips to the barn because he is now much stronger than I am, and three inches taller, too. Conservationists will pardon me, but I have even taught him how to attack trees. It has all been preparation for the moment when his college plays on national TV and he catches a short pass and then proceeds to run not around but *over* several members of the other team. And after he scores, he will turn to the network camera and stirringly say, "Hi, Mom."

9

Drowning
in Old Spice

Who Dressed This Mess?

The father of a daughter, especially one in her teens, will find that she doesn't like to be seen walking with him on the street. In fact, she will often ask him to walk a few paces behind. The father should not take this outdoor demotion personally; it is simply a matter of clothes. His are rotten. Every American daughter is an authority on fashion, and one of the things she knows is that her father dresses like somebody in the Mummers Parade.

In schools, you can always identify the children who were dressed by their fathers. Such children should have signs pinned on their strange attire that say:

Please do not scorn or mock me. I was dressed by my father, who sees colors the way Beethoven heard notes.

Whenever I travel with my kids, the moment I open my suitcase in a hotel, I see the instructions from my wife:

The red blouse goes with the gray skirt.

Do not let her wear the green striped shirt with the purple plaid pants.

The pink paisley pants and pink paisley sweater go together.

They may jog or sleep in their sweat suits, but no *one is to wear a sweat suit into the hotel dining room.*

The problem is that men are less studied than women about the way they dress. They never see what a woman sees—for example, that those khaki pants do not cover their ankles. Therefore, the child who goes out to be seen by the public represents the mother; and if this child is out of fashion, an observer will say, "Who dressed that little girl? Some woman at Ringling Brothers?"

"No," will come the answer. "That is Mrs. Cosby's child."

"You're kidding! In spite of her choice of husband, I've always thought that woman had taste."

"It must have been Bill who dressed the child today."

"Oh no, he's not allowed to dress them."

Unless he happens to work for Halston, the American father cannot be trusted to put together combinations of clothes. He is a man who was taught that the height of fashion was to wear two shoes that matched; and so, children can easily convince him of the elegance of whatever they do or don't want to wear.

"Dad, I don't want to wear socks today."

"Fine."

"Or a shirt."

"That's fine, too."

Mothers, however, are relentless in dressing children and often draw tears.

"Young lady, you are not going to wear red leotards

outside this house unless you're on your way to dance *Romeo and Juliet.*"

"But, Mom, everyone at *school* is wearing them."

"Then I'm helping you keep your individuality. You're wearing that nice gray skirt with the blue sweater and the white lace blouse."

"But, Mom, I *hate* that white lace blouse. It makes me look like a *waitress.*"

"Which is what you will be if you don't wear it 'cause you won't be leaving the house to go to school, and a restaurant job will be *it.*"

And now come the tears, which move a father deeply. His heart breaks for this child crying at seven in the morning, and he fears that this moment will leave a scar on her psyche. He wonders if Blue Cross covers psychiatry. Couldn't his wife back off a bit? After all, *he* would allow red leotards. He would *also* allow green combat boots.

However, a few minutes later at breakfast, where his darling little girl appears with swollen eyes, a runny nose, and the white lace blouse, she and her mother are getting along beautifully.

Of course, it is not hard to get along beautifully with my wife—certainly not for *me.* After twenty-two years of marriage, she is still as feminine as a woman can be; she has fine taste, especially in husbands; and we have many things in common, the greatest of which is that we are both afraid of the children. (The sternness with which she disciplines them is just a front.) I am happi-

est when she is happy, which means I am happy most
of the time.

No Hope on a Rope

Except on Father's Day. I am never as happy as I deserve to be on Father's Day. The problem is my presents. I trust my family to get them instead of simply
buying them for myself; and so, I get soap-on-a-rope.

In the entire history of civilization, no little boy or
girl ever wished on a star for soap-on-a-rope. It is not
the dumbest present you can get, but it is certainly
second to a thousand yards of dental floss. Have you
ever tried to wash your feet with soap-on-a-rope? You
could end up with a sudsy hanging.

Of course, soap-on-a-rope is not the *only* gift that can
depress a father on Father's Day: there are many others, like hedge cutters, weed trimmers, and plumbing
snakes. It is time that the families of America realized
that a father on Father's Day does not want to be
pointed in the direction of manual labor.

We could also do without a ninety-seventh tie or another pair of socks, and we do not want a sweater in
June. We appreciate the sentiment behind the buying
of the sweater: it was on sale; but we still would rather
have a Corvette.

Mothers do not permit Mother's Day to be run like this. Even General Patton would have lacked the courage to give his mother soap-on-a-rope. Mothers, in fact, organize the day as precisely as Patton planned an attack. They make a list of things they want, summon their children, and say, "Go see your father, get some money from him, and surprise me with some of these."

The kids then go to the father and say, "Dad, we need eight thousand dollars for some presents for Mom."

Mothers stress the lovely meaning of Mother's Day by gathering their children and tenderly saying, "I carried every one of you in my body for nine months and then my hips started spreading because of you. I wasn't built like this until you were born and I didn't have this big blue vein on the back of my leg. *You* did this to me."

For Father's Day, however, this woman comes to you and says, "It's one of those compulsory holidays again, one of those meaningless greeting-card things, so the kids are under pressure to buy some presents for you and the money is certainly not coming from *me*. Twenty bucks for each of them should do it—unless you'd rather have me put it on your charge."

You have five children, so you give her a hundred dollars. The kids then go to the store and get two packages of underwear, each of which costs five dollars and contains three shorts. They tear them open and each kid wraps one pair of shorts for me. (The sixth pair is saved for a Salvation Army drive.) Therefore, on this

Father's Day, I will be walking around in new underwear and my kids will be walking around with ninety dollars change.

Not every year, of course, do I get Old Spice or underwear. Many times a few of my kids are away from home on this special day, but they always remember to call me collect, thus allowing the operator to join in the Father's Day wishes too. I have, in fact, received so many of these calls that I'm thinking of getting an 800 number.

On Father's Day, which is almost as exciting as Ground Hog Day, I sometimes think of a famous writer named Dorothy Parker, who said that men were always giving her one perfect rose but never one perfect limousine. Well, I understand just how she felt. For just *one* Father's Day, I would like the kids to forget about the underpants, the tie, and the tin trophy saying WORLD'S GREATEST FATHER and instead surprise me with a Mercedes. Just put two hundred dollars down on it and I'll gladly finish the payments.

It will never happen, of course, because fathers are good actors who lie well. A father can sound convincing when he says that he is delighted to have another bottle of Old Spice because he is down to his last six. A mother, however, will refuse to accept such a bottle or a little tin trophy and will send the children back to the store to get it right. After all, it's the thought that counts. And did you kids think she was crazy?

On every day of the year, both mothers and fathers *should* be given more recognition than a jock or a trophy. I am still waiting for some performer to win an award and then step to the microphone and say, "I would like to thank my mother and father, first of all, for letting me live."

Academic Masquerade

Most fathers are such good people that they don't even mind having their wardrobes looted by the daughters they love, a point that brings us back to the subject of clothes. A few months ago, one of my sweaters disappeared; and then, two weeks later, another sweater disappeared, soon followed by a third. Were it not for my fourteen-year-old daughter's allergy to makeup, I would still be wondering what happened to those sweaters, or perhaps to my mind.

One day during that crime wave, my wife and I were summoned to school by the nurse because our daughter's face had suddenly swollen. Had she come down with the mumps in geometry? Or had she been attacked by killer bees? No, she had been attacked by the makeup she was putting on at her locker, the lipstick and eyeliner and blusher that she was secretly wearing at school to become a person I wouldn't have recognized. The other part of this disguise was a choice of my sweaters: her locker contained three of them, and one of my sports jackets too.

And so, I learned that part of my daughter's schedule at school was a fashion elective: every day she shed the drab clothes her mother had chosen and became Miss Supercool, with clothes that belonged to me and makeup I unwittingly had paid for when I'd thought I was giving her money for magazines.

On certain girls, this makeup looks like something out of a police lineup: funky stuff that complements pants rolled high above her socks, half-laced sneakers with holes artfully punched in them, and one of your sweaters with a shirttail showing below. She had to steal three of your sweaters, of course, because she certainly couldn't be seen wearing the same one two days in a row. But she still looks better in your clothes than you ever did, and you can't wait to kiss that grease-painted cheek.

10

Your Crap or
Mine?

Turn That Crap Down

Nothing separates the generations more than music. By the time a child is eight or nine, he has developed a passion for his own music that is even stronger than his passions for procrastination and weird clothes. A father cannot even convince his kids that Bach was a pretty good composer by telling them that he made the cover of *Time* a few years ago. The kids would simply reply that he isn't much in *People*.

"Okay," says the father grimly, standing at his stereo, "I want you guys to forget that Madonna stuff for a few minutes and hear some Duke Ellington."

"Duke Ellington?" says his son. "Is he a relative of Prince?"

Yes, the kids will listen to neither the old masters nor the great popular music that Mom and Dad loved in their own youth, the modern classics like "The Flat Foot Floogie" and the immortal ballads like "Cement Mixer (Put-ti Put-ti)."

When I was a boy, Patti Page made a record called "That Doggie in the Window." It swept the country, but it wouldn't sell ten copies today because it couldn't be filmed for a video. A cocker spaniel scratching himself in a pet store window lacks the drama a video needs, unless the dog were also coming into heat and fifty dancing veterinarians were singing, "Go, you bitch!"

Today's parents grew up with the silly notion that music was meant to be heard, that one picture was superfluous to ten thousand words. We now have learned, of course, that music has to be *seen*, that the *1812 Overture* is nothing unless you also see twenty regiments of Russian infantry. Duke Ellington was lucky to have done "Take the 'A' Train" when he did. If Duke were doing the song today, he would have to play it in the subway, with the lyrics being sung by a chorus of break-dancing conductors.

I doubt that *any* father has ever liked the music his children did. At the dawn of time, some caveman must have been sitting on a rock, contentedly whistling the song of a bird, until he was suddenly jarred by music coming from his son, grunting the sound of a sick monkey. And eons later, Mozart's father must have walked into the parlor one day when Mozart was playing Bach on the harpsichord.

"Turn that crap down," the father must have said.

And Mozart must have replied—in German, of course—"But, Dad, this stuff is *fresh.*"

The older generation is simply incapable of ever appreciating the strange sounds that the young one calls music.

One day last year, my daughter, who is eighteen now, came to me and said, "Dad, can I have ten dollars?"

As a typical father, I knew that I would be giving her the money; and, as a typical father, I also knew that I would be making her squirm before I gave it.

"What do you want it for?" I said.

"I want to buy a new album."

"A new album by whom?"

"The Septic Tanks."

When I was a kid, singing groups were named after such things as birds: we had the Ravens, the Robins, and the Orioles. But only the Vultures or the Pigeon Droppings could be singing groups today. And the lyrics are even worse than the names: these groups are singing the stuff that sent Lenny Bruce to jail. What my wife and I have always fondly known as sex is just foreplay today. Against a background as romantic as the Battle of Guadalcanal, these singers describe oral things that you never heard from your dentist.

The grotesque violence of some of these rock videos reflects a philosophy that many kids seem to hold:

"Well, it's *your* fault that everything will be destroyed."

But the kids have it *backward*. If they don't like the idea of destruction, then why don't they show us nymphs and shepherds merrily dancing on the grass instead of a guy who looks as though he is being electrocuted by his guitar?

About an hour after I had given my daughter ten dollars for her music, she came home with an album, and for the next twenty minutes I heard:

> *Slish-slish,*
> *Boom-boom,*
> *Slish-slish,*
> *Boom-boom.*
> *Grick, grack, greck*
> *And dreck.*

During this performance, the dog wandered in, glanced at the stereo, and sat down to listen. The dog loves this kind of music; he likes to breathe to it. At last, after the melody had segued to a noise that sounded like eruptions of natural gas, some singing began; and this singing was perfectly matched to the quality of the instrumental that had preceded it:

> *Oh, baby,*
> *Uhh-uhh, uhh-uhh.*
> *Come to my place*
> *And sit on my face.*

The Way It Was

When I was thirteen, my father used to sit in our living room and listen on our Philco radio to strange music by people named Duke Ellington, Count Basie, and Jimmie Lunceford. Sometimes when I walked by, I saw him leaning back in his armchair and smiling blissfully. My mission was to sneak *past* that living room before he caught me and made me come inside for a music appreciation lesson on the old-timey music that I couldn't stand.

"Come here and sit down," he'd say. "Now this is Jimmie Lunceford." He pointed to the Philco and smiled, while I tried to adjust my ears to the low volume. And when the piece was over, he'd say, "Now *that's* music. I don't know what you call the crap you hear upstairs, but *that's* music."

During each of these command performances, I would smile respectfully and move my head back and forth in rhythm as if I really enjoyed this junk; and after my own performance was over, I would pat my father on the knee, say, "Thank you, Dad," and tell him I had something important to do. The something important, of course, was to get away from that music. And then I would go upstairs and wonder how I could negotiate these walks past the living room and out of the house without having my father use his Philco to damage my brain. For a while, I considered putting a ladder against my window, but it also would have let a burglar in.

Had a burglar made it into my room, he would have had a wonderful time hearing Sonny Rollins, John Coltrane, Dizzy Gillespie, Miles Davis, Thelonious Monk, Bud Powell, and Philly Joe Jones. He would have been able to hear them right through any ski mask because I always played them at top volume. The greatest advantage of top volume was that I couldn't

hear the grownups when they came in to tell me to
turn that crap down.

From time to time my father would come by, kick
the door open, and then stand there under the assault
of the music. He had the look of a sailor standing on
deck in a typhoon. And then his lips would start to
move. I couldn't hear him, but I didn't have to, for he
was sending an ancient message:

Turn that crap down.

I then would turn the sound down about halfway,
moving him to say, "Turn it down, I said." I'd then
turn the dial to the three-quarters point and he'd say,
"More." Giving him more, I would say, "Dad, it's off."

"And that," he would say, "is what I want."

Music has changed so drastically since the days
when I first heard the wonders of John Coltrane and
Bud Powell. Today a guitar is a major appliance whose
volume guarantees that the teenager playing it will
never be aware of the start of World War III. This
teenager will merely see the explosions and will probably think that they are part of a publicity campaign for
a new English group called the Armageddons.

I know I don't sound hip talking like this, but no
matter *how* he talks, a father cannot sound hip to his
children. (I wonder if even the Duke sounded hip to
Mercer Ellington, or if Mercer just humored the old
man.) He can give high fives until his palms bleed; he
can say "Chilly down" so much that he sounds like a
short order cook; but the father will still be a man who
lost all his hipness at the age of twenty-three.

The day he started paying rent.

Remember Cosby's First Law of Intergenerational Perversity? Well, it also applies to being hip. Anything that *you* like cannot possibly be something your kids like too, so it cannot possibly be hip. You know what would end Madonna's career? If enough parents suddenly started to like her.

The Tender Trap

The volume of "that crap" is my own fault, of course. No one *made* me buy that complex stereo system for my decibel-hungry darlings. The day I went into the electronics store to see the equipment, those two BOX 95s and Bowie Twin Triple Hitter treble, woofer speakers, and double-headed action didn't *seem* too much for a twenty-by-fifteen bedroom, as long as there was no bed. I even failed to notice the gleam in my daughter's eye that resembled the gleam in Dr. Frankenstein's eye when he first decided to make a mobile. I had been too busy falling into the great American trap: trying to make a child happy by buying something for her.

If the children's name for me is Dad-Can-I, then my name for them is Yes-You-May. (My response is weak but *grammatical.*) You may have the tuner, the amplifier, the tape deck, and those two speakers that belong at a pregame rally at Grambling State. I must confess, however, that all this permissiveness was not entirely altruistic: I figured that whenever she wasn't home, I could rent her room as a recording studio.

And so I bought the stereo. The price was surrealistic, but what I got for my money was more than just equipment that belonged in Yankee Stadium: I got a smile that said that I was the greatest father in the world.

When I brought the equipment home, I simply opened the instruction book, which was slightly shorter than *Pride and Prejudice*, and flipped past the Chinese, Italian, French, and Turkish until I got to the English, which had been written by a foreigner. Only two hours later, the unit was assembled and I was issuing wise paternal advice:

"Now the thing to know is you needn't turn this unit up so loud. Leave the volume control on two and a half and your ears will adjust to every little nuance."

"Yes, Dad," my daughter said, still feeling that I was a wonderful person; and going to the stereo, she put on a record that sounded like a train derailment, which I pretended to like. I was trying to reach out to her generation, to understand that there might be more to music than just melody, harmony, and rhythm.

Then I went downstairs. A few minutes later, the doorbell rang (the first good music I had heard all day) and some of my daughter's friends came in. As I told them she was upstairs, I believe I heard one of them say that I was the greatest father since Abraham. And then, when they went upstairs, I sat down for lunch with my wife in the dining room, which is just beneath my daughter's bedroom.

Moments later, things began to move that ordinarily had no locomotion: the plates, the cups, the silverware, and the salt and pepper shakers.

"I was unaware," I told my wife, "that this house is sitting on a major geological fault."

When the chandelier began to swing and the chairs began to dance, I said, "If these are my last words, I want you to know only the greatest truth that is in my heart. I love you profoundly, and I never played halfback in that game against Penn."

While the glasses, plates, and utensils danced, my wife listened intently to a deep rhythmic thumping—two short thumps and one long one—that filled the house. And after listening to this extraterrestrial sound for about a minute, she turned to me and said, "That stereo is too damn loud."

You can see that I married above my IQ.

At once, I sprang into action. I rushed upstairs and kicked open the door to my daughter's bedroom like a man arriving at a fire. With the skin on my face feeling as though it were being pushed away from my skull, and with a vein struggling to free itself from the center of my forehead, the greatest father since Abraham cried the words that Abraham himself must have cried when Isaac brought home his new ram's horn:

"Turn that crap down!"

11

Unsafe
at Any Speed

Wheeler-Dealer

Buying a stereo is merely a father's practice for the Big Buy: a car. When his child requests a car, a father will wish that he were a member of some sect that hasn't gone beyond the horse.

"Dad, all my friends say I should have my own car," the boy says earnestly one day.

"Wonderful. When are they going to buy it?"

"No, Dad. They think that you and Mom should buy me the car."

"Is there any particular reason why we should?"

"Well, that's what parents *do.*"

"Not *all* parents. Did Adam and Eve get Abel a car? And he was the *good* one. Tell me this: why do you *need* a car?"

"To go places by myself."

"Well, you'd be surprised how many people manage to do that on public transportation. Elderly *ladies* do it every day. It's called a bus and I'd be happy to buy you a token. I won't even wait for your birthday."

"Dad, *you* know a bus isn't cool. My friends say I shouldn't have to ride on a bus now that I'm sixteen."

"They say that? Well, they couldn't be *good* friends

because buses are so much fun. They expand your social circle. You meet new people every three blocks."

"That's cute, Dad."

"I know you don't go particularly deep in math, but
do you happen to know what a car costs?"

"I'll get a *used* one."

"Terrific. And we'll have a family lottery to try to
guess the day it will break down."

"Okay, *slightly* used."

"Which is slightly more or less than five thousand
dollars, not counting insurance."

"Insurance?"

"You getting some used insurance too?"

"I'll drive it real carefully."

"And there's a chance you will," you say, suddenly
picturing people all over town bouncing off your son's
fenders.

"Dad, I just *have* to have a car. Say, what about
yours? Then you could buy yourself a *new* one. Dad,
you *deserve* a new car."

"That's very thoughtful, son," you say, now having
heard the ploy you've been expecting.

"Think nothing of it, Dad."

And so, the moment has come for you to gently remind your son precisely how worthless he currently is
—without bruising his ego, of course.

"You see," you tell him, "the thing is that unless a
wonderful offer came in last night, you have no job.
You are sixteen years old, you have no job, and you
have an excellent chance of failing the eleventh grade."

"Not *Driver's Ed!* I'm *creaming* that!"

"I'm happy to hear it. You'll go on to college—if we can find one in Baja California—and you'll major in Driver's Ed. Maybe you'll get your M.A. in Toll Booths and even your Ph.D. in Grease and Lube."

"Dad, I wish you wouldn't keep bringing up school. I'm just not motivated."

"To improve your mind, that is. But you *are* motivated to get a car. The bus may not go to the unemployment office."

"Come on, Dad; *you* know what a car means. I need it to *go* places."

"Like a fast-food joint, where your career will be. Because with the grades you have right now, if you somehow *do* happen to be graduated from high school, which the Vatican will declare a miracle, you'll be competing with only ten million others for the job of wrapping cheeseburgers."

"Dad, I'd love to talk more about my career, but I gotta tell you something really exciting that s gonna change your mind: I just saw an ad for a sensational sixty-nine Mustang."

"Really? How much?"

"Just two thousand dollars."

"Just two thousand dollars. Did you happen to ask if it had an engine? And are brakes optional?"

"Dad, I can't understand why you're being so unreasonable."

"That's what fathers are. It's one of the qualifications."

"But my friends keep saying I should *have* a car."

"And they certainly have the right to buy you one. I'll tell you what: how's *this* for reasonable? Bring your friends over here and we'll have a collection, a matching funds collection. Whatever you get from them, I'll match it."

The boy winds up with ninety-six cents.

Was That Me Driving By?

What I forgot to tell my son during this stimulating intellectual exchange was that my wife and I had already made a solemn decision about Cosby transportation: we would not allow any of the children to have a driver's license as long as he or she was living with us. Does this sound unreasonable to *you?*

One memorable day, one of these children *did* drive to town just to see if she could do it while unencumbered by a license. It was a Saturday morning and my wife and I had just finished breakfast. I walked over to the sink to rinse out a glass and there I suddenly saw our car going past the kitchen window. Turning to my wife, I said, "Dear, did you just drive by here?"

"No," she replied.

"Well, am *I* in this kitchen?"

"As far as I can tell."

"Then why did I just go by in the car?"

"You didn't," she said, moving toward the toolbox for something to tighten my screws.

A few minutes later, an idiot who happened to be my daughter came into the kitchen. I use the word idiot only in the narrow automotive sense, for my daughter is one of the brightest people her school has ever seen avoid work. In her defense, however, I must say that she does have a special philosophy about school: she feels that it is pointless to waste intelligence there.

"Dad, you didn't have to call me an idiot," she said after I had cooled off.

"That's true," I said. "But somehow the word seemed to fit."

"You don't understand. You just don't understand."

"No, I *do* understand. I just don't accept. Because when you drive with no license or insurance, you could run someone down, make him an instant millionaire, and send your mother and me back to the projects. And then you'll leave *us* because we won't be making enough money for you. And if you ever *do* get a driver's license, you know what they'll stamp on it? Legally stupid."

In Spite of Mutiny

Just as your children are not afraid to let you know that they are not perfect (they let you know it night and day), you must not be afraid to let them know that you're not perfect too. The most important thing to let them know is simply that you're there, that you're the one they can trust the most, that you're the best person on the face of the earth to whom they can come and say, "I have a problem."

If *only* more kids would say "I have a problem" instead of "No problem."

Your children have to know it's their responsibility to come to you when they are in trouble, even if it means their earning the title of idiot.

Let's say that you do buy a car for your daughter. It's an act of love and she is very happy to have it, both the love and the car. And you say, "Now I don't want anybody driving this car when they're drinking. In fact, I don't want this car to move with any hands on the steering wheel but yours. This car is not to be loaned like a sweater or a Duran Duran album, not even to go around the block. You could get hurt. And I could get sued for the trade deficit of the United States."

Now the rules have been set and the responsibility has been placed. But there is other pressure on the child too: the pressure of wanting to be liked. And so, it happens, and the moment has come for you to let the child know that something will be learned, though this is not your favorite school. And you also have to let the child know that there will be forgiveness, even when you hear the police say that liquor was involved.

"Look, kids do this," the police say.

"Yes, *other* kids," you say; "but we've *talked* about it."

Then you say to your daughter, "Didn't I *tell* you?"

And she replies, "Yes, but I didn't think . . ."

I didn't think.

If any words can describe the teenage years, these are the ones. A famous actor with two daughters once told me, "When a girl hits thirteen, you can just watch her lose her mind. Luckily, she gets it back; but during all the time that it's misplaced, you can lose your own."

In these trying years, as I have said, and can't say too often, a father just has to keep hanging around and loving and knowing that his baby needs guidance because her own rudder hasn't started working yet. To extend the nautical image, a father during these years has to do everything in his power to keep a tight ship, even though he knows the crew would like to send him away in a dinghy.

The Impossible Dream

Americans are often in love with their cars, so I'm not surprised when I travel around the country and find teenagers who would rather have cars than roofs over their heads. That is, the roofs they want are from General Motors.

For example, early last year, when I was performing at Lake Tahoe, I noticed a boy of about fourteen sitting quietly near the stage. He clearly wasn't enjoying the show, so I decided to bring him into it and then he'd be partly responsible for not having any fun.

Walking over to him, I said, "Son, do you like cars?"

"Oh, yes," he replied, perking up.

"What kind of car do you like?"

"A Corvette."

"And how much does a Corvette cost?"

"Around thirty thousand dollars."

"Tell me, how are you doing in school?" I said.

"Okay." The sweeping meaning of which you and I already know.

"You mean your grades are okay?"

"Well, uuhhh . . . some C's . . . and . ."

"Some C's and what? Some A's?"

"No, D's."

"In what were the D's?"

"Well, I got one in English."

"English? Were you born here?"

"Yes."

"And what language did your parents speak around the house?"

"English."

"And your newspapers were in English too?"

"Yes, they were."

"And television. Did your parents put on only Spanish or Bulgarian stations?"

"Oh, no."

Suddenly I was back on old familiar ground: another American boy whose native tongue was a foreign one.

"Okay, never mind that," I said. "So you got some C's and D's. Have you been told that you could do better?"

"Yes, I have."

"Teachers have told you that you're much brighter than your grades?"

"Yes."

"But you're just not motivated."

"That's right."

Once again, familiar ground. It sounds as though method acting has been brought to American schools. Before a child can play the part of a student, he has to say: *Well, what is my motivation here? Why am I doing this homework instead of hanging out at the mall? Can I look convincing going to class?*

"Okay," I said to the boy, "so let me see where you

are. Right now, you're somewhere below mediocre;
and as far as I know, there are not too many corporate
recruiters looking for a sub-mediocre person who
doesn't want to do anything. You see, you've got enormous competition for that position of not wanting to
do anything. By the way, do you have any real reason
for wanting a car?"

All right, all together now, let's sing out his answer:
To go places. How refreshing it would be if a child told
his father that he wanted a car for robbing banks.

And speaking of robbing banks, for the next few
minutes, I talked to the boy about raising the thirty
thousand dollars. I discovered he hadn't completely
worked out every detail of the financing. To distract
him from this pressure, I changed the subject and told
him a way to do his homework that had never occurred to him: read the assignments every night. And
then, at the end of my little commercial for scholar-
ship, I finally said, "Now, son, do you *still* think it's
important to have a thirty-thousand-dollar Corvette?"

"No," he said thoughtfully. "I think I'll go for a
Volkswagen."

12

The Attention
Span of a Flea

Remembrance of Things Upstairs

That boy at Lake Tahoe had trouble remembering the address of his school, but he is typical of young people. I have found that children remember only what they want to. It's a talent they develop from the very beginning.

For example, suppose you are sitting in your living room and suddenly realize that you need something from upstairs, but you feel too lazy to make the trip. Luckily, however, you have co-produced a five-year-old who goes upstairs just for fun and who also speaks your language. Moreover, at this moment, the child is in your very room, about to destroy an antique.

"Come here," you say to this child and she understands perfectly and moves directly to you. "I want you to get something from my bedroom and bring it down to me."

"*Sure*, Daddy!" the child says, delighted to be honored with such a mission. And this is why you are sending her: because the mission is an honor for her but would do nothing for you.

And now you tell the child not only the exact location of your glasses (on the table to the right of the bed), but also the exact location of your bedroom, as if she has never been in the house before. She is, after all, only five.

Within moments, however, you realize the child is having trouble remembering the difference between the left hand and the right.

"*This* hand," you say. "This hand is the *right* one, okay?"

"If you say so, Daddy."

"I want you to go to the table on Daddy's side of the bed, so here's what you do. Make this hand into a fist, hold it way out, and go upstairs. Leave it balled up in a fist so that when you go through the door, you can go in *its* direction. Won't that be *fun?* As much fun as chocolate cake for breakfast or taking a shower in your clothes. Now you do remember where our bed is, don't you? The one you like to come into when Mommy and I want to be alone."

"Uh-huh."

"Good! So you just go around to the side that's on the same side as your balled-up hand and then go to the table on that side. You know the one with the lamp on it?"

"Uh-huh."

"Well, my glasses are there. Bring Daddy's glasses right down here. Now what did I say?"

"Go upstairs to your room and look on the table," says the child. "With the right hand balled up."

"You are going to do brilliantly on the SATs. Just bring those glasses down to Daddy."

"Okay."

And so, you return to your reading, trying to guess what the words are because your glasses have not yet arrived. After a while, you sense that too much time has passed since you sent the child for the glasses; and then you see this very child walking past your living-room chair, but she says nothing to you. She is simply walking around, so you call her over and say, "Sweetheart, I thought I asked you to get my glasses."

And the sweetheart says, "Oh, yeah. Uh, I didn't see them."

Drawing her closer, you say, "Did you go up to my room?"

"Yeah."

"My room in *this* house?"

"Yeah."

"And you looked on the table?"

"Yeah."

"And you didn't see them?"

"Yeah."

"With your hand balled up?"

"Yeah."

"Okay, now you just go back upstairs and look on that table nice and hard because I know I left them there."

"Well, Dad, I didn't see them. I looked for them and I didn't see them."

"Did you look on the *other* table?"

"No."

At once, you're aware of your own stupidity in not having asked the child to look on both tables. And so, you say to her, "Sweetheart, go up again. Keep your hand balled up on that side and look for the glasses. Keep your *hand* balled up, but nothing else."

And the child goes upstairs again, and this time she comes back, so definite progress has been made.

"They're not there, Dad," she says.

"You definitely looked on the other table?"

"Yeah."

And so you lead the child upstairs. Both of you have your right hands balled up because this is a learning experience.

"Now we put our hands straight out," you tell her as you enter the bedroom, "and we follow them like this."

And there, on the table, are your glasses.

You start to get angry, but you cannot sustain it, for how can you be angry at a child who is so pretty and biteable? Sustaining anger at a biteable daughter has been a father's timeless problem. I doubt it can ever be solved.

"*Here* are my glasses," you say. "I thought I *told* you they were here."

"But, Dad," she sweetly replies, "they weren't here when I *looked* for them."

"You came over to this side?"

"Yeah."

"And you looked?"

"Yeah."

"And they weren't there?"

"No, Dad. Not there at all."

There are many times during the fathering years when you wonder about the condition of your mind, and this is one of them. I don't think *anyone*, not even a magician or a psychic, could have said whether or not those glasses were on the bedside table when the child went up to look for them. The psychic might have told you, "I see this as a great learning experience."

And she would have been right: you have learned to get your glasses by yourself. Moreover, your child has learned a little something about remembering directions. It may take several more trips to fetch things before her mind will be as well trained as a golden retriever's, but you will keep trying. You will keep trying and keep having patience.

And *that* is fatherhood.

Be It Ever So Rent Free

Your reward will be that some day your daughter will come home to you and stay, perhaps at the age of forty-three. More and more children these days are moving back home a decade or two after they have stopped being children because the schools have been making the mistake of teaching Robert Frost, who said, "Home is the place where, when you go there, they have to take you in." Why don't they teach *You Can't Go Home Again* instead?

I recently met a man and woman who had been married for fifty years and they told me a story with enough horror for Brian DePalma. Their forty-six-year-old son had just moved back in with them, bringing his two kids, one who was twenty-three and one who was twenty-two. All three of them were out of work.

"And that," I told my wife, "is why there is death."

Who wants to be seven hundred years old and look out the window and see your six-hundred-year-old son coming home to live with you? Bringing his two four-hundred-year-old kids.

I have five children and I love them as much as a father possibly could, but I confess that I have an extra bit of appreciation for my nine-year-old.

"Why do you love her so much?" the other kids keep asking me.

And I reply, "Because she's the last one. And I never thought that would occur. If I'm still alive when she leaves at eighteen, my golden age can finally begin."

I find there is almost music to whatever this child does, for, whatever she does, it's the last time I will have to be a witness to that event. She could set the house on fire and I would say, "Well, that's the last time the house will burn down."

She is as bad as the others, this nine-year-old; in fact, she learns faster how to be bad; but I still look at her with that extra bit of appreciation and I also smile a lot because she is the final one.

I sympathize with the older ones for not under-

standing. They are perplexed because things they did
that annoyed me are now adorable when done by the
nine-year-old. When the older ones took pages from a
script I was writing and used them for origami, I was
annoyed; but when the last one does it, I feel good all
over.

After their last one has grown up, many fathers
think that the golden age of solitude has arrived, but it
turns out to be fool's gold, for their married children
have this habit of getting divorced; and then they drop
off the children at your house while they go to find
another spouse.

And sometimes it is not only the children but animals too.

"Dad, I wonder if you could watch our horse while
we're away."

"Well, what if your mother and I decide to go someplace?" you say.

"You people are *old*. You don't *go* anywhere."

The only reason we had children was to give them
love and wisdom and then freedom. But it's a package
deal: the first two have to lead to the third. Freedom—
the thing so precious to Thomas Jefferson. He didn't
want *his* kids coming back either, especially because he
had *six* of them.

In spite of all the scientific knowledge to date, I have
to say that the human animal cannot be the most intel-
ligent one on earth because he is the only one who
allows his offspring to come back home. Look at anything that gives birth: eventually it will run and hide.

After a while, even a mother elephant will run away from its child and hide. And when you consider how hard it is for a mother elephant to hide, you can appreciate the depth of her motivation.

Look Homeward, Sponger

When you and your wife are down to one child and that child is nineteen, when you are in the home stretch of the obstacle course that is leading you to the golden years, *never* buy a bigger house. And if, for reason of insanity, you do buy one, make sure that it's in Samoa or else the children will see it and say, *"Look! They're there!"* Moreover, some of these children have studied biology and know you're going to die, so they express the kind of feeling that is found in the major poets:

"Whoever's in the house when they die, gets it!"

For generations, fathers have been telling sons who are nearing the end of their college days, "Son, your mother and I don't care *what* career you finally decide to pursue because the important thing is that you will be going forth."

The key word here is *forth*. Every time you attend a graduation, you hear a dean or president say, "And so, young men and women, as you go forth . . ."

For years, I had thought that forth meant going out into the world on their own; I had thought that forth meant leaving home. But then I discovered that I was wrong. Every time that they go forth, they come back, so forth must mean home.

My father, however, gave to forth its old traditional meaning. On the day I was graduated from college, he presented to me a Benrus watch and then he said with a smile, "All right, now give me the keys to the house."

"Why, Dad?" I replied.

"Because you're going forth, which is any direction but to this house."

But I got my mother to let me back in.

"He's just a baby," she said.

This baby lived with his parents until he was twenty-four years old. It was a good life: food was free, there was hot and cold running water, and my laundry was done—eventually. It took a while to have my laundry done because my hamper was the floor of my room. I learned what many young men have learned: if you leave your clothes on the floor of your room long enough, you can wait your mother out. Sooner or later, she will pick them up and wash them for you. The price you pay will merely be her noisy disgust:

"All these stinking, moldy clothes . . . just a disgrace . . . at twenty-four . . . he must think I'm his slave . . . he must think I want to start some kind of *collection* of rotting clothes."

Fathers, however, are a little tougher about such earthy living. My father set my clothes on fire.

"Unfit for man or beast," he said. "Not even fair to the *garbage* men to make 'em handle stuff like that."

After I had been living at home for a while at the age of twenty-four, my mother and father had a meeting about me and they decided to charge me rent. The figure they chose was seven dollars a week; and I considered this figure fair because I was producing forty dollars' worth of laundry.

Once I began paying rent, I had the right to tell my mother that she wasn't doing this laundry well enough for my sartorial style.

"Now look, Mom," I said, "if you want this seven dollars a week, then you've got to improve your work on these collars. If I ever want to *wear* a damp one, I'll tell you."

I really took advantage of those people; but if you can't take advantage of your mother and father, then what do you have them for?

I have known parents who are even harder on adult child boarders than mine were, parents who charge their children as much as eleven or twelve dollars a week. Sometimes this money has to come from the adult child's allowance, thus creating the financial version of a balanced aquarium.

"I'm telling you now, you're gonna pay us rent," the father says. "You're gonna give us twelve dollars a week."

"Don't worry, you can skip the week of your birthday," the mother says.

The best thing about living at home is the way your

parents worry about you. Of course, they have *reason* to worry about you. They know you.

I.O.U. Aggravation

The flow of money between generations always seems to be a problem in American families. Now that my father is a grandfather, he just can't wait to give money to my kids. But when I was *his* kid and I asked him for fifty cents, he would tell me the story of his life: how he got up at four o'clock in the morning when he was seven years old and walked twenty-three miles to milk ninety cows. And the farmer for whom he worked had no bucket, so my father had to squirt the milk into his little hand and then walk eight miles to the nearest can. For five cents a month.

And I never got the fifty cents.

But now he tells *my* children every time he comes into the house, "Well, let's just see if Granddad has some money for these wonderful kids."

And the moment they take the money out of his hand, I call them over and take it from them. Because that's *my* money.

13

Ivy-Covered
Debt

Hail to Thee, Bankruptcy

I was wrong when I said that the big expense for you would be buying a car. Let us now discuss the cost of college—unless you would rather do something more pleasant, like have root canal work.

As you know, I have always put the highest value on education. However, one day last year, my eighteen-year-old daughter came in and told my wife and me that she had decided not to go to college because she was in love with a boy named Alan.

At first, my wife and I went crazy.

"What?" I cried. "You're standing there and telling your mother and me that you're *not* going to—"

And then a light went on in one of the musty corners of my mind: her decision would be saving me a hundred thousand dollars.

"—not going to college, which you have every *right* to tell us. Alan, you say? Well, he just happens to be the one I'm exceptionally fond of. I hope he's feeling well. Would you like me to send him to Palm Beach for a couple of weeks to get a little sun?"

A father like me with five children faces the terrifying prospect of sending five to college. When my oldest one went, the bill for her first year had already reached thirteen thousand dollars. I looked hard at this bill and then said to her, "Thirteen thousand dollars. Will you be the only student?"

I am lucky enough to make a lot of money; but to the average American father today, thirteen thousand dollars (which has now gone up to seventeen) is more than just a sum of money: it is the need for a winning lottery ticket.

When I saw my oldest daughter's first college bill, I multiplied thirteen thousand times four, added another thirty thousand for incidentals during these four years, and got the sum of eighty-two thousand dollars that I would be spending to see my daughter pick up a liberal arts degree, which would qualify her to come back home.

You think I'm exaggerating that extra expense for incidentals? For her freshman year, I had to spend another seventeen hundred for a tiny room just a quarter mile from a toilet. And then the college said that if my wife and I really cared for our child, we would pay another three hundred for the gourmet special. We wound up sending another five hundred to our daughter personally so that she would not have to eat the gourmet special but could get pizza instead.

"Dad, the food is terrible," she kept saying.

"But I enrolled you in *gourmet* food," I said.

"That's worse than the other. I want pizza."

And then, on top of the five hundred dollars a year that we sent for pizza, we also had to keep flying her home because her clothes kept getting dirty. She was studious, so she was unable to remember to wash her clothes. She simply flew them home every few weeks and put ten thousand dollars' worth of laundry into our washing machine.

At this college, my daughter did not major in mathematics. *No* children learn mathematics at college, even when they take the courses; I have never met a college student who knows how to count. You give one of them a certain amount of money and a budget precisely broken down to cover all her expenses.

"This is for this," you say, "and this is for that."

The child listens carefully and calls you forty-eight hours later to say she is broke.

"And, Dad, the telephone company is being really *unreasonable*."

"Did you pay the bill?"

"We're certainly *planning* to. And *still* they want to turn it off."

"But I *gave* you enough—there's money in your *budget* for the telephone bill."

"Oh, we used that money for important things."

In my daughter's sophomore year, one of these important things was housing: she and her roommates decided that they just had to have their own apartment. They no longer could stand living in the dorm, where the shortsighted dean had objected to their putting up pictures of naked people playing guitars.

I discovered these pictures on a surprise visit, which I had made to tell my daughter that her mother and I loved her, wanted her to work hard, and were behind

her all the way. Upon entering her room, I expected to
see pictures of little kittens playing with thread, but
instead I saw a young man who looked as though he
was making music at an Army physical. My daughter,
of course, was not supposed to be majoring in anat-
omy.

You Could Major in Spackling, Too

The eighty thousand dollars that you will be spending
for college might not leave you quite so depressed if
you knew that the school's curriculum were solid. I am
afraid, however, that the curriculum has turned to cot-
tage cheese.

When I went to college, I sometimes cut classes to go
to the movies; but today the movies are the *class*—
sorry, The Film Experience. There are also such challenging courses as The History of Western Belching,
the Philosophy of Making Applesauce, and Advanced
Lawn Mower Maintenance. It is no surprise to hear a
college student say on his graduation day, "Hopefully,
I will be able to make an input. College was a fun time,
but hopefully now I'll have a viable interface with software." The software is his *brain*. The degree he is truly
qualified to be given is one in Liberal Semi-Literacy.

I do not mean to sound stuffy or old-fashioned. I just

feel that for eighty thousand dollars a student should spend four years in a school where English comes up from time to time. I cannot stand to see it being scaled *down* to the students. The students should be reaching up to *it* because success in life demands the use of intellect under pressure. Also knowing how to spell.

A freshman today will change his schedule if he finds he has signed up for a course that requires books. He wants courses that will enable him to both sleep late and get rich, so he will test his intellect with such things as The Origins of the Sandbox, American National Holidays, and the Principles and Practices of Billing.

I have mentioned my feeling about grade school teachers who keep saying, "He can do the work," my feeling that if only one of these teachers would call the boy a certified idiot, I would say, "Fine; we'll get someone to work with him." Well, in college the teachers don't say, "He can do the work." They say, "What kind of work would he like to do?" And it is this new trend of letting students shape their own curriculum that leads a student to tell his advisor, "I'd like to study the number of times every day that the average light at an intersection turns green. I want to major in Traffic."

14

Full-Time Job

In from the Cold

Some authority on parenting once said, "Hold them very close and then let them go." This is the hardest truth for a father to learn: that his children are continuously growing up and moving away from him (until, of course, they move back in). Such growth is especially bittersweet with a daughter because you are always in love with her. When she is very small, she comes to you and says, "Daddy, I have to go to the bathroom," and you proudly lead her there as if the toilet were a wedding chapel. You drop to your knees, unbutton her overalls, and lovingly put her on the seat.

And then one day it happens: she stops you from unbuttoning her and pushes you away because she wants privacy in the bathroom. It is your first rejection by this special sweetheart, but you have to remember that it means no lessening of her love. You must use this rejection to prepare yourself for others that will be coming, like the one I received on a certain day when I called my daughter at college. Someone in her dorm picked up the phone and I asked to speak to my daughter. The person left and returned about a minute later to say, "She says she's sleeping right now."

I was hurt to have my daughter put me on hold, but intellectually I knew that this was just another stage in her growth; and I remembered what Spencer Tracy had said in *Father of the Bride:* "Your son is your son till he takes him a wife, but your daughter is your daughter for all of your life." You are stuck with each other, and what a lovely adhesion it is.

There is no commitment in the world like having children. Even though they often will drive you to consider commitment of another kind, the value of a family still cannot be measured. The great French writer André Malraux said it well: "Without a family, man, alone in the world, trembles with the cold."

Yes, it is even better to have Jeffrey, that wee airborne terror, than to have no child at all. Just make sure that you travel in separate planes.

This commitment, of course, cannot be a part-time thing. The mother may be doing ninety percent of the disciplining, but the father still must have a full-time acceptance of all the children. He never must say, "Get these kids out of here; I'm trying to watch TV." If he ever does start saying this, he is liable to see one of his kids on the six o'clock news.

Both mother and father have to work to establish an *honesty.* The child doesn't have to tell them *everything,* but he *should* be talking to his parents the same way he talks to someone who is not in charge of his life. When your son has his first wet dream, you don't want him to have it interpreted in the boys' locker room. And if your daughter's period is late, you want her to feel as comfortable going to you as to a confidante at the mall.

Sometimes I tell my son that the meaning of his name is "Trust nobody and smile." But that certainly doesn't apply to his parents: my wife and I have tried to stay tuned in to him and the girls from the very beginning. We have shown all five of them constant attention, faith, and love. Like all parents since Adam and Eve (who never quite seemed to understand sibling rivalry), we have made mistakes; but we've learned from them, we've learned from the *kids*, and we've all grown together. The seven of us will always stumble and bumble from time to time, but we do have the kind of mutual trust that I wish the United Nations had. And, with breaks for a little hollering, we smile a lot.

Afterword

by Alvin F. Poussaint, M.D.

Bill Cosby makes fatherhood come alive. He takes us on a comedic yet insightful journey through the awesome shifting sands of parenthood. Along the way, he selects for emphasis those stages of fatherhood through which most men, who elect to participate actively in the great spiritual and psychological adventure of parenting, must pass.

The experience of fatherhood begins, as Cosby notes, long before the birth of your first child. It then passes through the stages of infant, toddler, preschool, school-age, preteen, teenager, and adult. There are new, different, and challenging issues at each stage of development that parents must face and resolve. These stages frequently merge and overlap, producing significant individual variations. Parents are also changing, developing, and experiencing their own life stages as their children grow. The child/parent interactions at any given stage, therefore, are more complex than it at first appears.

Because of the new interest in the role of fathering, a significant body of information, gathered by scholars and laymen alike, has shed new light on the most effective approaches to the different stages of fatherhood. Bill Cosby, in beginning this book, warns: "I doubt there can *be* a philosophy about something so difficult, something so downright mystical, as raising kids." To a large degree he is correct.

Child-care experts caution us that there is no single "right" approach; much variation exists in successful parenting styles. In addition, the mores of one's culture, religious orientation, country, community, and family influence the kind of role mothers and fathers assume in child-raising. Relatively speaking, there is no such thing as a perfect father any more than there is a perfect mother. All parents make mistakes and in most instances children can successfully overcome their caretakers' shortcomings if they are raised in a loving, caring, and disciplined environment.

Let us begin, then, at the point at which Bill Cosby starts this book: expectant fatherhood ("So you've decided to have a child."). Most men decide to be fathers for similar reasons that women want to be mothers: to reproduce themselves and undertake the challenge and fulfillment of successfully raising and interacting with a child from birth to adulthood. Men who elect to be participatory fathers look forward to the birth of a child with the same sense of anticipation, joy, doubt, and anxiety as most expectant mothers.

Both old observations and new research have shown that the expectant father, particularly one who gives it no forethought, begins his journey when he learns his partner is pregnant. From this point on for the duration of the pregnancy, the expectant father, besides his own reactions, is affected by the experiences that his partner undergoes as the pregnancy progresses to reach its endpoint: the birth of a baby.

Pregnancy is divided conveniently into trimesters, each with its special qualities, pleasures, and discomforts for the woman, to which the man responds. During the first trimester, women may experience "morning sickness," during which they feel nauseated and may vomit. They often feel fatigued, bloated, and may have a variety of minor physical complaints as their body changes to accommodate the developing baby. Their moods may vary from joy to depression, depending on their previous mental state or their current feelings about being pregnant. Often pregnant women at this stage may report that they feel vaguely "different" because of the many psychological and physiological changes they are undergoing.

The father-to-be during this period must be supportive and patient with his partner, while also realizing that he is experiencing joy, excitement, and nervous-

ness of his own. He must respond to not only his
wife's pregnancy, but also his own vicarious reactions
to her pregnancy. He may feel proud, boastful, and
even powerful because his "manhood" is being demonstrated by his own fertility. A few may experience
"sympathetic" pregnancy symptoms because of strong
identification with their pregnant spouse. Yet the reality of the pregnancy may cause many men to anx-
iously assess their own preparedness for fatherhood
and its accompanying responsibilities. For the expectant couple the beginning of pregnancy can be an exciting mix of stress, sharing, and joy.

In out-of-wedlock pregnancies, such anxieties cause
some men to panic and then flee to avoid both the
financial and the psychological responsibilities of
parenting. Some males, unfortunately, are interested
only in impregnating a woman to become a biological
father and have no interest in becoming a psychological father: a man who helps to raise and support his
children. Fathers who willingly abandon their offspring are shortsighted and irresponsible. They short-
change their children, their families, society, and
themselves. Absent fathers, due to whatever cause, are
missing the opportunity for an unparalleled form of
self-fulfillment and emotional satisfaction, including
involvement in their partner's pregnancy.

For participating fathers, the second trimester
brings another set of experiences that make the baby
seem much more of a reality. The first movements of
the baby can now be felt. Bill recalls when his wife

woke him up in the middle of the night and yelled: "It's moving; wake up and feel it!" These movements are called "quickening" and the parents are now convinced that there is something "alive and kicking in there." The expectant father should participate in feeling the baby move. But men should be aware that, even though it may feel great to them, the movements of the baby sometimes may be uncomfortable for the mother. Yet the father's sharing of the experience will help him to understand and empathize more appreciatively with his wife's responses.

The last trimester brings new excitement but new stresses as well. Mother's abdomen is growing large and protruding. There is considerable weight gain, about twenty to thirty pounds. Often women experience "puffiness," swollen ankles, insomnia, and an aching back. Physical movements become awkward and, as Bill Cosby indicates, simply getting up and sitting down may become an ordeal for the pregnant woman. Women—and their mates—may be filled with worries about the normality and health of the baby. Thoughts about the sex of the child become prominent, as do the many preparations for her or his arrival. Sexist attitudes may surface if the father goes overboard in his preference for a son and implies that girls are not worth as much. Attitudes of this type in either parent may be disturbing to the other.

As the day of delivery approaches, fathers may worry about their sexual needs and are anxious to consult their physicians about when to abstain. Men also fret about the details of getting their partner to the hospital when labor begins. Bill describes the chaotic excitement that characterizes this event in the beginning of this book. Once in the hospital, birthing center, or attended at home, the experience of the delivery looms as a deep and lasting experience for both mother and father.

Not many decades ago, fathers were not permitted in the delivery room. Today, this has changed. Many couples attend courses on labor and delivery so that they can share and experience the birth together. Husbands are able to assist their wives, comfort them, and participate in the birth in the delivery room. A family feeling is established, and both mother and father can begin to bond immediately with the child.

The adjustment to the new baby causes some stress as home routines and styles change in response to baby's demands. For men who are confused or in conflict about their role as fathers, this is a critical time. If they are traditional, they may retreat and leave all or most of the custodial tasks such as feeding, bathing, and diapering to the mother. Traditional mothers, also, may try to push men away from these "feminine" chores and conflicts may result. To avoid misunderstandings, it is important for the couple to discuss and decide on their respective "feminine" and "masculine" roles and responsibilities *before* the baby arrives.

Fathers who want to bond closely with their babies should share in caretaking. As Bill says, "For a new father, this little person is something he can hold and love and play with and even teach, if he knows any-thing." Bill mentions many humorous getting-to-know-you incidents that occurred while he was en-gaged in such routine activities as feeding and dressing his children. It should reassure any male readers grow-ing anxious at this point that the new fatherhood movement sanctions such activities as "masculine." There is no cause here for men to worry about their manhood.

Paternal participation in caretaking offers enormous support to the mother and strengthens the bonds be-tween the couple. When older children are in the fam-ily, the father can also play an active role in helping his children cope with the new baby and their own periodic feelings of jealousy, displacement, and sibling rivalry. He can also assist them in engaging in helpful activities with their new sibling. This kind of father involvement is especially important because a new and tired mother is often not as available as before to her other children. A daddy can fill the gap!

Today, there are more and more men taking time off from work, or requesting paternity leave, to spend this critical early period learning parenting tasks expected of the modern father. Fathers, by the way, are often just as interested in and delighted with their newborns as the mother. Indeed, there are many occasions when Dad is more "high" on the baby than Mom, because Mom, having gone through the physical stress of the delivery, may be feeling more exhausted than "high." (A word of caution: fathers should not get so wrapped up in their baby that they neglect their relationship with their wives.)

As the baby begins to grow, besides the custodial care required, fathers can take an active role in helping their children in social, physical, and intellectual development. This is best accomplished during the activities that are considered play. Fathers who are less androgynous in their orientation may feel more comfortable in playing games and reading to their young ones than in changing their diapers and dressing them. They should make use of toys and games that aid in their child's exploration of his or her environment. Dads also enjoy holding, touching, rocking, and lifting their children. These physical games and exercises are important for a child's motor development and coordination. Fathers who think they should get involved only when they can begin to teach their child (usually the son) sports are way off base. Child-care specialists report that early involvement of parents in stimulating play with their youngsters facilitates their growth.

Modern fathers must try to check inclinations to "rough house" with their sons and not with their daughters. All games and sports are as appropriate for girls as they are for boys. Child-care experts have strong evidence that restrictive and often damaging sex-role typing begins early in infancy and is perpetuated in many subtle ways by fathers—and mothers. It is worthwhile for fathers and mothers to reflect periodically on their attitudes toward male and female roles. Through self-examination they may avoid personal biases that impede their sons' and daughters' healthy development.

Divorced and out-of-wedlock fathers should realize that constructive involvement with their children is an important ingredient in shaping their offspring's growth and identity. Psychological fathers in all categories serve as role models who can significantly influence their children's personalities and development. Fathers, for instance, can contribute greatly to the management of the preschool and school-age child.

Children going off to school marks a major transition for parents. When Bill and I were boys, this took place at age five, when we went to kindergarten in the public schools. It is different today. Because of changing family patterns—more women in the work force, and growing numbers of single-parent families—there has been a great need for child-care services outside of the home for very young children. Adding to this pressure for services is the belief by some parents and teachers that formal education and socialization outside the home should begin sooner than age five.

As a result, more and more children are beginning "school" in the form of Head Start, day-care, and nursery school at ages two and three. There are even day-care centers that specialize in infant and early toddler care. Many have educational programs that occasionally go overboard in "hurrying" children's development. Some experts criticize programs that utilize high-pressure, "flash card" educational techniques to produce "super" children. Parents should scrutinize such programs to be sure their youngster is not being needlessly overstressed.

For many fathers and mothers, involvement in a child's "school" activities begins earlier than in the past. Because working parents often have conflicting schedules, fathers and mothers have to juggle their schedules to get their children ready for school, drop them off, and pick them up. Modern fathers who take an active interest in their children's progress are involved in exploring school programs, meeting with teachers, and dealing with educational problems as they arise. For instance, both parents should review report cards; praising, scolding, and counseling should be, when possible, a joint affair. In the past, many school duties were performed solely by the mother. A father's participation not only eases a mother's burden, but benefits the school-age child as well.

Some fathers may begin to identify more closely with their sons when relating to the older school-age child (age five to six) and wish to be role models and guides for them. This is healthy as long as Dad is not neglecting or rejecting his daughters, or sex-typing them into limited roles and opportunities. Fathers can be very helpful during this stage. Children of elementary-school age love outings, trips, and exploration. They also have great curiosity and are generally anxious to know more about their environment. Trips to the grocery store are an opportunity to educate them about money and arithmetic. Trips to a restaurant are a chance to teach social skills. Outings to movies and museums can be just plain fun for both children and father and have educational value.

Fathers who work should explain to their growing youngsters what kind of job they perform. They can bring their child to their workplace so that they can see this other world where Daddy, or Mommy, participates. In the old days it remained a mystery to many children exactly what their fathers did when they "went to work." Fathers will seem less remote when children are not left in the dark about their parents' outside activities.

Children ask many questions at elementary-school age, including questions about sex. The old practice of fathers referring these questions to mothers is no longer acceptable. Fathers should, with their daughters as well as sons, respond to such intimate questions in a manner appropriate to the child's age. Preteens will frequently have questions, particularly about the sexual development of their bodies. Bill mentions that he would want his son to talk to him if he has questions about "wet dreams" and he would want his daughters to express any worries to him about a missed period. This open attitude will lay the groundwork for children to talk more comfortably about intimacies and feelings with father as well as with mother.

Some fathers, unfortunately, hold back expressions of affection to their challenging children of school age because they fear that it might interfere with their "strong" image and diminish their effectiveness as a stern disciplinarian. Fathers who are too stern and too often play the role of the whiplasher make their children too frightened of them. This interferes with a comfortable father/child relationship. Parents do not have to frighten children excessively or make threats of violence to make them obey.

Bill Cosby, in some of his comic material, refers to whacking his son on the behind on one occasion and getting good results when other approaches had failed. There is much controversy surrounding spanking as a means of discipline. There is, nevertheless, much anecdotal material that suggests that corporal punishment of children is an effective form of discipline. Even the old adage states: Spare the rod and spoil the child. Parents, however, too often use spanking to vent their own frustrations and anxieties. In such cases, spanking becomes an attack on their children and not a genuine attempt at constructive discipline.

Most psychiatrists and psychologists discourage the use of violence in any form to discipline children. On the other hand, there are times when children can be so exasperating that most parents will lose control and give their child "a good whack." If this happens occasionally to loving parents, there is no reason to feel excessive guilt. There is no evidence that it produces psychological harm unless the "whack" is of the force to constitute child abuse. Fathers who physically harm their children must be legally restrained at the same time that they seek counseling to prevent future abusive behavior.

Parents will be most effective in getting obedience

from their youngsters by explaining the reasons why certain behavior is not allowed. And often these lessons have to be repeated again and again to children, so patience is required. Modern mothers should avoid casting the father as a would-be child executioner. Fathers can best participate in discipline by recognizing that rewards and punishments for good and bad behavior are more likely to produce the desired result than a spanking. Most child specialists recommend the reward/punishment style of discipline mixed with consistency and love. Praise a child for desired behavior and reprimand or ignore a child displaying unacceptable behavior. Saying, "Go to your room and don't come out until you can behave," may be more productive, and certainly less painful to father and child, than a beating.

To better manage some of these frustrating discipline issues, father should be in harmony with mother on disciplinary techniques and should not allow a child to pit them against one another and manipulate them. Cosby satirically deals with these issues in much of his comic material and is correct in trying to motivate his children to behave without his playing the role of Bill the Policeman.

Wise parents know that good discipline in a child's early years prevents some of the headaches that come when their child reaches adolescence, which is about age twelve these days. Adolescent children can be especially difficult for fathers who have had an unbending, tough attitude about absolute obedience. Teenagers normally challenge and frequently rebel against the authority of their parents as they move toward greater independence and realization of their own adulthood.

Teenagehood is a time that calls for the maximum of parental flexibility and patience. A father might find himself faced with a previously obedient and compliant child, or at least one who had quietly gone about accepting Dad's word as law, suddenly telling him to "Go chuck it!" Fathers who respond too harshly, or who try to beat teenagers, may find themselves hit back by them or may soon have a young runaway. Teenagers feel a great sense of indignity when parents try to use physical force to discipline them. Again, reason and the use of rewards and nonviolent punishment is the best approach.

Parents have to be ready to take some adolescent challenges as a matter of course and allow teenagers to make as many of their own decisions as possible, so long as they do not endanger their own well-being or the well-being of others. Adolescents usually like to experiment and "try out things" for themselves. They are not as likely to "take your word for it" as they were as children. Some of their activities and challenges to the father's authority may reawaken conflicts in the father—and mother—about sex, drugs, smoking, and different forms of behavior. If a father believes his teenage son or daughter is moving in a direction away from his—the father's—expected aspirations, he may become anxious as well as angry. Failures at school or "hanging out with the wrong crowd" may be particularly exasperating to fathers who feel that, as the "head of the household," they should be in control.

One of the tasks for a father during his child's progression through adolescence is to give up more and more control at the same time that he tries to guide his teenage child in the right direction. But, as Bill Cosby recognizes in his presentations, there is a contradiction and conflict here: adolescents are usually still economically dependent on their parents, particularly the father if he is the primary breadwinner. The attitude of many fathers is: I'm taking care of you, so you do what I say. The implied afterthought is: If you don't like it, move out.

This approach will work to some degree, but it may also drive a strong wedge between the adolescent and Father, simply because the teenager does not want to feel totally controlled by him or Mother, particularly with the threat of withdrawing financial support. Many will take on the challenge, run away, live in the streets, and eventually get into all kinds of dangerous and unlawful activities just to spite Dad and Mom.

It is important, at this stage of development, to help adolescents reach independence in constructive ways. Foremost, fathers should maintain an active interest in their teenager and not retreat because they are feeling a sense of angry impotence. Teenagers, despite their disclaimers, need strong parental involvement and will appreciate it in later years. Secondly, opportunities to participate in decision-making along with sharing some adult responsibilities such as helping maintain the household should be available to them. This includes having part-time jobs, taking on major household chores like cooking and cleaning, and deciding on how they would like to spend their summer vacation. The object is to reward adult behavior and to remain as patient as possible when childish acting-out aggravates you. Adolescents will at times make unrealistic demands and are very ambivalent about their real dependence on their parents. That they have to ask parents for things, particularly money, is a constant reminder that they are not yet independent adults.

Adolescents, even those with part-time jobs, will need money from their parents for clothes and other items. Bill Cosby jokes frequently about the demands of adolescent children for clothes, cars, and other luxuries. This is certainly a real issue and the challenge is to satisfy some of their needs when possible but not to overindulge them. Whenever possible, adolescents should be required to contribute to purchases of large items such as stereos and cars. Bill moans that the more he buys his kids, the more they seem to want. Many parents would agree with him. On the whole, fathers should be willing to give, particularly when it supports the responsible growth of their budding adult.

Some adolescents will become independent earlier than others. There are those who drop out of high school to work, others who graduate from high school and go to work, and those who go on to college to drop out or to graduate. Among these varied patterns, parents should remember that many adolescents may be "late bloomers." There are many stories of adolescents who early on seriously foundered but significantly achieved at a much later age.

College-bound children are financially dependent and, if their children go on to graduate or professional school, parents may be supporting a child into their mid and late twenties. Fathers in intact homes who are primary breadwinners, and single fathers and mothers, may be particularly burdened with what seems to be the never-ending financial burdens of parenting. Indeed, economic times being as hard as they are, some grown children may be returning home to live if the parents allow it.

Just as a father feels it is all ending and his children are off to start their own families, a new role begins. In mid-life, Dad may experience his second "fatherhood" as a grandparent. Bill Cosby playfully reminds his own children that someday they will be parents and he will sit back and chuckle as they struggle with their children in the same way he struggled with them. "I just hope that when you get married, you have children who act just like you."

Grandfathers do have a special place in the lives of their children's children. They can delight and play with them and even indulge them in ways that they did not indulge their own children. Grandfather knows that after the fun and games are over with his adorable grandchildren he can return to the quiet of

his own home and peacefully reflect on this phenomenon of fatherhood.

Bill Cosby's willingness to share many of his own
fatherhood experiences in this book will encourage
men everywhere to participate more actively in
parenting. Though this volume is titled *Fatherhood*, its
effect will be to strengthen the entire family. Bill, who
has relentlessly demonstrated his concern for kids,
knows: Strong families raise strong, healthy children!